Merton
& Waugh

A MONK,
A CRUSTY OLD MAN
& *THE SEVEN STOREY MOUNTAIN*

Mary Frances Coady

PARACLETE PRESS
BREWSTER, MASSACHUSETTS

2015 First printing
Merton and Waugh: A Monk, A Crusty Old Man, and The Seven Storey Mountain

ISBN 978-1-61261-628-5

The Paraclete Press name and logo (dove on cross) are trademarks of Paraclete Press, Inc.

Library of Congress Cataloging-in-Publication Data

Coady, Mary Frances, author.
  Merton and Waugh : a monk, a crusty old man, and the seven storey mountain / Mary Frances Coady.
    pages cm
  Includes bibliographical references.
    ISBN 978-1-61261-628-5 (hardback)
  1. Merton, Thomas, 1915–1968. 2. Waugh, Evelyn, 1903–1966. 3. Merton, Thomas, 1915–1968—Correspondence. 4. Waugh, Evelyn, 1903–1966—Correspondence. 5. Merton, Thomas, 1915–1968. Seven storey mountain. I. Title.
  BX4705.M542C63 2015
  271'.12502—dc23
                                    2014041901
10 9 8 7 6 5 4 3 2 1

Published by Paraclete Press
Brewster, Massachusetts
www.paracletepress.com

Printed in the United States of America

Contents

The extant correspondence of Thomas Merton and Evelyn Waugh, from August 2, 1948, to February 25, 1952, comprises twenty letters: thirteen from Merton and seven from Waugh.

Merton's letters were written on paper containing variations of the letterhead "Gethsemani Abbey, Trappist, Kentucky." One was handwritten and the rest typed. Waugh's letters were handwritten on paper with the letterhead "Piers Court, Stinchcombe, Gloucestershire," which was his home address. Waugh seems to have had a systematic method for saving others' letters to him, but Merton—at least at the beginning of his fame as a writer— had no such system, and it is only because of the archival instinct of his friend Sister Thérèse Lentfoehr, who, Merton notes in one letter, "has a misguided notion that I am the cousin of Santa Claus," that any of Waugh's letters to the Trappist monk managed to be saved at all.

In the transcription of the correspondence included in this volume, the dates of the letters have been standardized and the year has been added in square brackets to letters where it had been omitted. Both writers had stylistic idiosyncrasies in writing the titles of books and magazines, sometimes indicating them in capital letters, sometimes underlining, sometimes not making them stand out at all. These have also been standardized with the use of italics, while the truncated form of the titles that each of the correspondents often employed has been kept. Merton had trouble with the spelling of certain words ("succede" for "succeed," "discrete" used improperly for "discreet"); these have been corrected. In a few places missing words have been placed within square brackets. Likewise, a few commas have been added to certain passages for greater clarification.

The Waugh Estate has allowed no more than two-thirds of each letter from Waugh to Merton to be printed. Ellipses indicate the omissions. Five of these letters can be found almost in their entirety in the *Evelyn Waugh Newsletter/ Studies* (Vol. 3 No. 1), via the website of The Evelyn Waugh Society (http://evelynwaughsociety.org/journal/). Thanks to Luke Ingram and Thomas Dobrowolski.

In 2009 I received a Shannon Fellowship from the International Thomas Merton Society, which enabled me to spend several days working on the Merton/Waugh material at the Thomas Merton Center at Bellarmine University in Louisville, Kentucky. Thanks to Paul Pearson and Mark Meade for answering my many questions there. Thanks as well to Paul Spaeth of the St. Bonaventure University Archives in St. Bonaventure, New York, who allowed me access to the Naomi Burton Stone Collection, and to the Merton Legacy Trust for permission to quote from two of Merton's letters to Naomi Burton Stone. I am also grateful to John McGinty and Jeff Manley, and to John H. Wilson, editor of *Evelyn Waugh Studies*.

Thomas Merton's letters to Evelyn Waugh first appeared in *The Courage for Truth: The Letters of Thomas Merton to Writers*, edited by Christine M. Bochen, and published in 1993. I am grateful for the permission to reprint these letters. Likewise, grateful acknowledgment to Houghton Mifflin Harcourt for permission to quote passages from *The Seven Storey Mountain*.

Part of the present book was worked on during the summer of 2012 at the Collegeville Institute for Ecumenical and Cultural Research in Collegeville, Minnesota, and I am grateful to both the institute and the Lilly Foundation for a tranquil week of writing.

Finally, I owe much gratitude to Jon Sweeney, Robert Edmonson, copyeditor Jeff Reimer, and the staff of Paraclete Press.

"I came into the world"

In the early summer of 1948, the British novelist Evelyn Waugh, low in spirits because of unrelenting rain and an itchy nettle rash, received a manuscript in the mail from an American publisher, along with a request for an endorsement. Waugh was newly famous in America; two years earlier, his novel of illicit love and divine grace, *Brideshead Revisited*, had been named a Book of the Month Club selection, and as a result became a national bestseller. Previously little known, the novelist was now a writer of note, especially among educated American Catholics.

Waugh himself had a jaded view of Americans; a visit to the United States the year before had ended badly. His opinion of his own country was little better, however. He detested not only the gray weather but also the high taxes and postwar rations imposed by the British government. The unsolicited package from the United States, containing the galley proofs of an autobiographical book by an obscure Trappist monk who lived in rural Kentucky, proved a distraction for him. Waugh read the pages and sent the publisher an immediate reply.

The title of the soon-to-be-published book was *The Seven Storey Mountain*. The editor who had sent Waugh the proofs was Robert Giroux of the New York publishing company Harcourt Brace. The company's president was uncertain about whether a book by a Trappist monk would sell, and so Giroux, in an effort to give it prominence, had sent the text to several well-known Catholic writers with the hope that at least one would respond with a quote-worthy endorsement. Besides Waugh, three others received galleys of the book: Graham Greene, Clare Booth Luce, and Bishop Fulton J. Sheen. Giroux did not expect to hear from Waugh, but when he received the novelist's reply— as well as praise from the other three—he increased the print run from 5,000 to 12,500 copies.

The Seven Storey Mountain was published a few months later, and Waugh's endorsement was chosen for the cover of the first edition: "I regard this as a book which may well prove to be of permanent interest in the history of religious experience. No one can afford to neglect this clear account of a complex religious process." The name of the author was Brother Louis, but the cover of the book would carry only his birth name: Thomas Merton.

The Seven Storey Mountain covered ground that Evelyn Waugh was more or less familiar with in his own life—early precociousness, desire to become a visual artist, a dissolute youth spent at a one of England's great universities, serious emotional setbacks in early adult relationships, a drift toward a literary career, and finally, conversion to Catholicism. The Catholic Church in which Merton was received in 1938 offered solace and a moral and religious structure to rein in the wildness in his temperament, as it had for Waugh eight years earlier. But there was even more drama in Merton's life story: a childhood odyssey that took him from his 1915 birth in the south of France to bohemian artist parents and his mother's early death, back and forth across the Atlantic to Long Island, New York, and to England, losing his father to cancer at the age of fifteen. The removal of this slight anchor led him, as a scholarship student at Cambridge University, into a year of debauchery that ended in what seems to have been a paternity suit. A final move across the Atlantic that began in his sense of shame brought him to the heady, vibrant world of New York City, where he made life-changing friendships and discovered the Catholic faith. And then, at the age of twenty-six, three years after his conversion, he entered the Cistercian Order of the Strict Observance (otherwise known as Trappists), a rigorous religious order that emphasized silence and asceticism.

Waugh was not entirely uncritical in his praise of *The Seven Storey Mountain*, however. He found a few faults with the book—the monk-author was too hard on Cambridge University, and his writing was verbose and diffuse. The essential message of twentieth-century conversion and religious experience, Waugh thought, was in danger of being drowned out. The book needed a good editor.

～ひ

Unknown to Waugh, the manuscript of *The Seven Storey Mountain* had already been reduced from a sprawling tome of nearly seven hundred pages to just over four hundred. It was not Merton's first book. In fact, the monk had been writing almost from the day he walked through the gate of Gethsemani Abbey in Kentucky on December 10, 1941. When he entered the Trappists, Merton had been prepared to give up writing completely in order to follow a higher calling, only to find that the abbot of the monastery, Dom Frederick Dunne, was a bibliophile whose father had been a bookbinder and publisher. The abbot was also in charge of a community of nearly two hundred monks. The abbey was in debt, the buildings in serious disrepair, and in need of some means to fill the coffers. Although the Trappists' main work was manual labor, there was already a literary precedent at Gethsemani. Father Raymond Flanagan's book, *The Man Who Got Even With God*, the biography of a Texas rebel who became a monk, had been published the year Merton entered the monastery. Flanagan's book became a favorite among Catholics, and just as important, it brought royalties and donations to the monastery. It was not long before Merton, too, was put to work at a typewriter.

Thus the abbot unwittingly highlighted a conflict within Merton that would never quite be resolved. After he left Cambridge University in disgrace and enrolled at New York's Columbia University for the 1935 winter term, Merton had displayed a literary flair almost immediately. He became part of a cutting-edge artistic group and submitted articles, poems, and drawings for the university's humor magazine, *The Jester*. He received his master's degree in English in 1939 and began writing autobiographical novels, two of which he presented to Robert Giroux, who had been a classmate at Columbia and had by now become an editor. Giroux saw evidence of talent in the emerging writer's work, but neither manuscript proved successful as a novel. The structure of each was too loose, the characters were derivative of those of Hemingway, and the style was too self-consciously that of James Joyce. Reacting to these rejections, Merton concluded that the novel was "a lousy art form anyway."[1]

In spite of his desire to begin his life anew, there was still a writer lurking inside Merton. Even as he bade goodbye to his former life and entered the monastic enclosure in 1941, having destroyed most of his writing, he left some manuscripts, including an unpublished novel, with his former professor and mentor at Columbia University,

Mark Van Doren. (The novel, lightly autobiographical, which he called *The Journal of My Escape from the Nazis*, would be published much later as *My Argument with the Gestapo*.[2]) He brought a few poems with him into the enclosure, eventually showing them to the abbot, who encouraged him to continue writing poetry. As the months went by, he found himself composing more poems, and he sent these, along with the ones he had brought with him, to Mark Van Doren. In 1944, eight months after he made his simple monastic vows, the poems were published as a collection by New Directions under the title *Thirty Poems*. It was Merton's first book.

In 1946 a second book of Merton's poems, *A Man in a Divided Sea*, was published. By the end of that year he had written a series of monastic guides for Trappists and pious pamphlets for the monks and the retreatants who came to the monastery. He also completed two biographies of Trappistine nuns, which were nearly ready for publication. These would become *Exile Ends in Glory*, the biography of Mother Berchmans, the foundress of a monastery for Cistercian women in Japan; and *What Are These Wounds?*, a life of St. Lutgarde, a twelfth-century Flemish mystic and stigmatic.

On March 1 of that year, he had written to his New Directions publisher, James Laughlin, of a new project—"creative, more or less poetic prose, autobiographical in its essence, but not pure autobiography. Something, as I see it now like a cross between Dante's *Purgatory*, and Kafka, and a medieval miracle play."[3] It had been "brewing" for a very long time, he added. He hoped he could keep it relatively short, about a hundred and fifty pages. The book-in-progress already had a name: *The Seven Storey Mountain*, after the ascent of the soul as it is purified of the seven deadly sins in Dante's *Purgatorio*.

By late summer, the project had become much more straightforward: "no fantasy, no Kafka, no miracle play. It is straight biography, with a lot of comment and reflection, and it is turning into the mountain that the title says."[4] An even more explicit description of the book appeared in a document written by a so-called anonymous monk of Gethsemani who sought the approval of the Chapter of Cistercian Abbots convening in France that year: "the biography or rather the history of the conversion and the Cistercian vocation of a monk of Gethsemani. Born in Europe, the son of artists, this monk passed through the abyss of Communism in the university life of our time before being led to the cloister by the merciful grace of Jesus."[5]

In the fall of 1946 Merton sent the manuscript of *The Seven Storey Mountain* to Naomi Burton, of the agency Curtis Brown, Inc., in New York, who had become his literary agent in the years when he was trying to get his novels published. Five years earlier, upon learning of his entry into the silent monastic cloister, she had lamented that she would never hear from him again. She now replied with enthusiasm for the manuscript. He received her letter on December 13, the feast of St. Lucy, patron saint of light, the fifth anniversary of the day he had been formally accepted into the Trappists. Naomi Burton told him she was sending the manuscript to Merton's classmate-turned-editor, Robert Giroux. This was by far his most blatantly personal piece of writing yet—the text representing the purging of his soul. There was no telling what Giroux, who had rejected his novels, would think about this more intimate work.

He recorded in his journal that when he was handed a telegram from Robert Giroux in the refectory on December 28, "my heart sank into my dinner." He thought at first that the manuscript had been lost. And then he remembered that his agent had sent it to Giroux only a week earlier. Publishers always took weeks and even months before commenting on a manuscript submission. The message was likely to be an out-of-hand rejection. He waited until after dinner before opening the telegram. It said simply, "Manuscript accepted. Happy New Year."[6]

Like all Merton's written work, the text of *The Seven Storey Mountain* had to pass through the Cistercian censors. There was shock at some of the passages, in particular those that described the author's sexual encounters as a young man, possibly including references to the paternity suit that had ended Merton's studies at Cambridge University. These were excised, and only oblique references were left to describe Merton's premonastic sexual adventures. Readers would either have to fill in the blanks for themselves or assume that late-night drunkenness was the full extent of the author's debauchery. One censor, whom Merton's journal identifies as Father Gabriel, went further, objecting to Merton's writing style, which he considered inferior. He suggested that Merton take a correspondence course in grammar. (Merton was much gratified later on when the abbot general on a visit from Rome told him it was fine to write slang, which he considered his most natural prose style.)

For Giroux, some parts of the censored text still contained editorial problems. There was too much abstract sermonizing, and the writing tended to be long-winded. This was a criticism Merton readily agreed with, acknowledging that long-windedness tended to be a literary fault of silent Trappists who found themselves tapping the keys of a typewriter. The manuscript began with four pages of wordy discourse, the first sentence reading: "When a man is conceived, when a human nature comes into being as an individual, concrete, subsisting thing, a person, then God's image is minted into the world." For Giroux, this kind of writing would produce yawns, and he told Merton that readers of an autobiography would want to know immediately who the author himself was.

After a few attempts, Merton came up with a sentence that ranks among the most memorable first sentences in English literature: "On the last day of January 1915, under the sign of the Water Bearer, in a year of a great war, and down in the shadow of some French mountains on the borders of Spain, I came into the world." The sentence sings as a kind of chant as the phrases roll lyrically toward the final five-word statement of the author's birth. The time, "a year of a great war" and the place, "the borders of Spain," establish gravitas and European worldly wisdom. The insouciant "down in the shadow of some French mountains"—as if the author cannot be bothered to write "Pyrenees"—adds a touch of American nonchalance. The sentence is a near-perfect introduction to a book that promises literary depth, irony, and the unfolding of the author's dramatic life story.

By the end of April 1948, Merton was correcting the page proofs. Bound copies of *The Seven Storey Mountain*, with Evelyn Waugh's endorsement on the cover, were delivered to bookstores in August.

1

"The enthralling task"

What was it about *The Seven Storey Mountain* that elicited Evelyn Waugh's excitement and praise? As a student in Oxford, Waugh had mocked religious ritual while becoming increasingly attracted to it. In the first flush of fame as the author of two celebrated novels, *Decline and Fall* and *Vile Bodies*, he became a somewhat reluctant Catholic in 1930 at the age of twenty-seven after receiving instructions from the Jesuit Martin D'Arcy. "I realise that the Roman Catholic Church is the only genuine form of Christianity," he had written to Father D'Arcy a few weeks earlier. "Also that Christianity is the essential and formative constituent of western culture. In our conversations and in what I have read or heard since, I have been able to understand a great deal of the dogma and discipline which seemed odd to me before." The only problem, he said, was that "I don't feel Christian in an absolute sense. The question seems to be—must I wait until I do feel this—which I suppose is a gift from God which no amount of instruction can give me, or can I become a Catholic when I am in such an incomplete state and so get the benefit of the sacraments and receive Faith afterwards?"[7]

Waugh's friends later speculated that his world was in chaos during that period of his life because his wife had deserted him, and he was wandering homeless from one friend's country house to another. Catholicism's discipline and ritual helped keep the turmoil in check. His inner world had always contained a terrifying disorder that erupted in savagely comic novels and in a misanthropic attitude, bordering on cruelty, toward others. What impressed Father D'Arcy was that at the time of his conversion Waugh, a divorced man, thought he would never be able to remarry and have children, and yet he was willing to make this sacrifice. (He would later receive an annulment and remarry.)

Also, although Waugh regarded Catholicism as a bastion against the modernity he eventually came to detest, especially after the Second World War, more profoundly he saw the church's teaching on prayer and charity exemplified in the lives of the saints. These became a guide for his own practice and behavior, and he knew that he came up woefully short at every turn. His Christian charity, however, came through in generous donations to struggling church organizations and articles for such Catholic publications as *The Tablet* and *The Month*, for which he received very little remuneration.

Waugh's novel *Brideshead Revisited,* published in 1945, brought him renewed fame. He described the book as an attempt to show the action of divine grace on a particular family. It was a wealthy, aristocratic Catholic family, and creating characters within this milieu revealed Waugh's predilection for that kind of society. Beyond that, however, it indicates a certain kind of Catholic Church in Waugh's imagination—on the one hand, an all-or-nothing Catholicism, and on the other, a Catholicism that embraces everyone, from the steely mother, steadfast oldest son, and pious schoolgirl, to the renegade father, wayward daughter, and alcoholic younger son. All are God-haunted in some way, but God's mercy is shown particularly to the family's outcasts.

When *Brideshead Revisited* was selected by the Book of the Month Club for January 1946, its popularity introduced Waugh to a new phenomenon: American fan mail. He was appalled by the questions in readers' letters, which he considered impertinent and overly personal. Had he always wanted to become a novelist? Were his characters based on real people? Was there to be a sequel to *Brideshead Revisited*?

Life, the prominent American magazine of photo-journalism, climbed on the Waugh bandwagon and sent a representative to his home in the county of Somerset with the suggestion that *Life* produce a photographic feature on him and his novels. Waugh tetchily refused on the grounds that he wanted no more to do with American popularity. As a compromise, he wrote an article called "Fan-Fare," which was published in the April 8, 1946, issue of *Life*. The article, both curmudgeonly and enlightening on matters such as his approach to writing ("I start [fictional characters] off with certain preconceived notions of what they will do and say in certain circumstances but I constantly find them moving another way."[8]), answered the questions he had received from American readers who had become enthralled with *Brideshead Revisited*.

In the wake of the novel's romance and baroque setting, it was not long before Hollywood called, and in January 1947, the MGM studio arranged for Waugh and his wife, Laura, to make their first trip to the United States for the purpose of negotiating movie rights. Waugh's tendency to regard all things American with contempt was at an all-time high. Even before *Brideshead Revisited*'s popular success and its trail of fans, "American" to Waugh suggested the embodiment of tastelessness, vulgarity, and shallowness. This trip did not alter his attitude. Ill-humored, he arrived in sunny and casual California wearing his Englishman's stiff white collar and bowler hat, and carrying an umbrella. He became even more irritated when he met the screenwriter who was to turn *Brideshead* into a film and discovered that the man regarded the story simply as a romantic tale, devoid of religious meaning. The movie deal fell through, but Waugh found unexpected, fertile imaginative ground in the garish Forest Lawn Cemetery. As a result of his California experience, his article "Death in Hollywood" appeared in the September 1947 issue of *Life*, and became the background of his eventual comic novel *The Loved One*. He returned to England in the spring, less enamored of the United States than ever.

The galley proofs of the unknown American Trappist's autobiography that landed in his mail in the early summer of 1948, however, revealed another side of America to Waugh. He had no sooner read the proofs and sent off his endorsement than he got in contact with Clare Booth Luce, a former Congresswoman and high-profile Catholic convert, who was also the wife of Henry Luce, the founder and editor-in-chief of *Life* magazine. He proposed that Waugh write an article on the American Catholic Church for *Life*. He was now convinced that American Catholics were going to be important for the future of worldwide Catholicism. American monasticism, as described by the young monk-author, seemed to be flourishing, and indeed, Waugh thought, it might even save the rest of the world. (Merton himself had already become critical of the self-satisfaction in American Catholicism and his own

monastery's busyness and machinelike atmosphere that
militated against contemplation. When word of Waugh's
optimism for Catholic America reached him, he wrote in
his journal—unaware that his own writing had largely
contributed to the British novelist's new enthusiasm—
"This is all news to me."[9]) Waugh, sensing an opportunity,
decided to make another trip to the United States.

Then, still in the glow of excitement over newly
discovered American Catholicism, Waugh agreed to edit
The Seven Storey Mountain for publication in Britain. On
August 28, he wrote in his diary, "Tom Burns[10] gave me [the]
enthralling task of cutting the redundancies and solecisms
out of Tom Merton's *[The] Seven Storey Mountain*. This
took a week and has resulted in what should be a fine
thin volume."[11] The ironic use of the word "enthralling"
suggests that the job of cutting through Merton's prose
was done for little or no remuneration, an act of homage
to a new religious voice. Also, despite Waugh's fervor, the
editing job was uninspiring and exasperating.

In the meantime, Merton's American publisher had
sent him Waugh's letter with its words of praise for *The
Seven Storey Mountain,* as well as its criticisms of the
book.[12] Merton was not yet aware that Waugh was to
be the editor of the British edition, but he certainly knew
Waugh as a writer. He had first come upon Waugh's novels
as a teenager in England in the 1930s. On his first visit

to Gethsemani, in the spring of 1941, he had had several hours' wait in Louisville and spent it in the public library reading Waugh's book about his travels in Abyssinia, *They Were Still Dancing*, which Merton greatly admired. And now in front of him was critical feedback on his own work from this great master of English prose. Before Merton heard directly from Waugh himself, he wrote a letter to the novelist. He had found himself in a literary quandary, and who better to ask for help than a Catholic literary giant?

Dear Mr. Waugh,

You will be surprised to get this but not, I hope, annoyed. Father Abbot gave me permission to write to you when I saw your letter to Harcourt Brace about *The Seven Storey Mountain*. I was especially grateful to get your reactions to the book in terms of an English audience and it is about that and all its implications that I feel this letter ought to be written.

About the Cambridge passage, I felt the same way afterwards, thought of rewriting it. My agent, who is English, said it was okay, so I let it stand. Then every time it came up in proof I worried about it, but was too lazy to do anything definite. The book is already printed here. But I'd like to clean up that Cambridge section a bit for the English edition which some people called Hollis and Carter are doing next spring. Do you think people would accuse me of duplicity in saying one thing here and another there? Anyway, I'm not as mad at Cambridge as that either. About the succinctness—perhaps the book should have been rewritten. A tremendous amount of dead wood was cut. But there was no time to go over the whole thing again. The poem was the idea of the editor at Harcourt Brace (I suppose you mean the one about my brother[13]) and not mine. I tried to get it out but did not succeed. It is too late now, at least for the American edition. I'll probably have to go by what the English editor thinks, on that.

The real reason I write to you is not merely to re-hash these little details. I am in a difficult spot here as a writer. Father Abbot gives me a typewriter and says "write" and so I cover pages and pages with matter and they go to several different censors and get lost, torn up, burned, and so on. Then they get pieced together and retyped and go to a publisher who changes everything and after about four years a book appears in print. I never get a chance to discuss it with anybody and scarcely ever see any reviews and half the time I haven't the faintest idea whether the thing is good or bad or what it is. Therefore I need criticism the way a man dying of thirst needs water. Those who have any ideas in their head about writing and who can communicate with me by letter or word have so far told me that I need discipline. I know. But I don't *get* it. A man can do something for himself along those lines by paying attention and using his head, I suppose. But if you can offer me any suggestions, tell me anything I ought to read, or tell me in one or two sentences how I ought to comport myself to acquire discipline I would be immensely grateful and you would be doing something for my soul. Because this business of writing has become intimately tied up with the whole process of my sanctification. It is an ascetic matter as much as anything else, because of the peculiar circumstances under which I write. At the moment, I may add, I am faced with a program of much writing because we have to raise money to build some new monasteries and there is a flood of vocations. Most of what I have to do concerns the Cistercian life, history, spiritual theology, biographies etc. But, (be patient with me!) consider this problem: all this has suddenly piled up on me in the last two years and I find myself more or less morally obliged to continue connections with the most diverse kind of publishers. On one end of the dilemma I am writing poetry and things like that for New Directions and a wacky surrealist magazine called *Tiger's Eye* that I think I had better get out of.

In the middle is Harcourt Brace. Next year they are bringing out a book I have done about our Order and the life and so on.[14] Then Sheed and Ward wants something—an expansion of a pamphlet I did for the monastery and which might interest you, so I'll send it along. Finally, at the other end is Bruce and Co, popular Catholic publisher in Milwaukee, and, of all things, a magazine called the *Messenger of the Sacred Heart* which has just gone through a reform and has elevated itself above the level of *True Story* and *True Romances* to become a kind of pious *Saturday Evening Post*. But I only did one article for them—no more. Then *Commonweal* is always on my neck asking for things.

Frankly, I think the devil is trying to ruin me. And I am left more or less on my own in all this. I have got to find some kind of a pace that is steady and disciplined and uniform and pretty near the top of whatever I may be capable of, and stick to that—then if they all want to buy some of it they can.

You see by this that it is a real problem, and a spiritual one too. Of course the whole thing may change with my being taken out of this job and put on something else after I am ordained, which should come next year. We are short of men all round. But I have been bold enough to impose on your patience and your charity because I have always considered you to be about the best living writer we've got. You do not need to be told that if you read the *Seven Storey Mountain.* I think I have read *Decline and Fall* and *Vile Bodies* over more than any other book except perhaps *Ulysses:*[15] I mean before coming here. Needless to say I am very thankful for your notice which the publisher intends to use on the jacket of the book.

I shall certainly pray for you and hope you will pray for me too.

In Corde Christi,

Frater M. Louis Merton O.C.R.

*

2

"Faults of style are largely faults of character"

SEPTEMBER – OCTOBER 1948

One wonders what Waugh thought of the American monk's letter, which reads like youthful outpouring of pent-up frustration to a father confessor. Mark Van Doren no longer served as a mentor, and thus Merton did his writing in isolation, with no fellow writer to discuss literary problems. In the spiritual universe he lived in, his writing and his prayer life were bound up together, and he was caught in a vortex, pulled down by the mix of self-recrimination, the abbot's expectations, the clamoring of editors wanting his work, the monastery's busy routine, and his own inability to fine-tune his own writing. It hardly exemplified Waugh's vision of the grand new flowering of monasticism.

Waugh replied just over a week later, not revealing that he himself was the "English editor." He readily accepted Merton's request for advice, and—after gamely giving the nod to monasticism, ignoring Merton's three-ring-circus description of his own monastery—he did not mince words.

Dear Brother Louis[16]

. . . My criticisms were really personal. . . . With regard to Cambridge: we don't at all mind criticism of our institution. We rather relish it. But I felt that your criticism rebounded on yourself. I wanted to answer: "You wasted your opportunities at the University and are trying to put the blame on it instead of on yourself."

In the same way I didn't like your criticisms of the Franciscans. God knows I have no business to lecture other people about charity, but I expect a higher standard from professed religious than from myself. I think you could have shown that you had no vocation as a friar without suggesting that friars were rather inferior people.

One other criticism of subject matter. I think for the full truth of your story you should have made it clear—tho of course quite dryly and briefly—how far your various "love" affairs were carnal and how far purely sentimental. This is of course a matter of great delicacy in which your superiors may have ruled you. But this information is lacking and I think it is needed.

With regard to style. It is of course much more laborious to write briefly. Americans, I am sure you will agree, tend to be very long-winded in conversation and your method is conversational. I relish the laconic. This is a personal preference and there is not the smallest reason for you to respect it. . . .

. . . I fiddle away rewriting any sentence six times mostly out of vanity. I don't want anything to appear with my name that is not the best I am capable of. You have clearly adopted the opposite opinion . . . banging away at your typewriter on whatever turns up.

. . . But you say that one of the motives of your work is to raise money for your house. Well simply as a matter of prudence you are not going the best way about it. In the mere economics of the thing, a better return for labour results in making a few things really well than in making a great number carelessly. You are plainly undertaking far too many trivial tasks for small returns.

I believe writers such as yourself and Christopher Hollis[17] fall into an excess of modesty about your own work which you would not approve in, say, a watchmaker. It is easier to make a good watch than write a good book. You wouldn't think much of a man who was content with anything which ticked and revolved.

Your superiors, you say, leave you to your own judgment in your literary work. Why not seek to perfect it and leave mass-production alone? Never send off any piece of writing the moment it is finished. Put it aside. Take on something else. Go back to it a month later and re-read it. Examine each sentence and ask "Does this say precisely what I mean? Is it capable of misunderstanding? Have I used a cliché where I could have invented a new and therefore asserting and memorable form? Have I repeated myself and wobbled round the point when I could have fixed the whole thing in six rightly chosen words? Am I using words in their basic meaning or in a loose plebeian way?" . . . The English language is incomparably rich and can convey *every* thought accurately and elegantly. The better the writing the less abstruse it is. Say "No" cheerfully and definitely to people who want you to do more than you can do well.

Alas, all this is painfully didactic—but you did ask for advice—there it is.

Yours sincerely,
Evelyn Waugh

In an effort to help Merton clean up his prose, Waugh sent him a copy of *The Reader Over Your Shoulder*, by Robert Graves and Alan Hodge, which had been published five years earlier. This book contained commentaries on such matters as the confusion that results from combining official language with colloquialism (for which Waugh was to later admonish Merton). It also held forth with several chapters on principles of syntax ("It should always be made clear who is addressing whom and on the subject of whom.") No mark of punctuation was outside the authors' purview ("The Dot," "The Asterisk"). Merton copied out a line attributed to the writer Arnold Bennett, which presumably struck a personal chord with him: "Faults of style are largely faults of character."

Dear Mr. Waugh,

I cannot tell you how truly happy I am with your letter and the book you sent. Both of them have been a very great help to me. In case you think I am exaggerating, I can assure you that in a contemplative monastery where people are supposed to see things clearly it sometimes becomes very difficult to see *anything* straight. It is so terribly easy to get yourself into some kind of a rut in which you distort every issue with your own blind bad habits—for instance rushing to finish a chapter before the bell rings and you will have to go and do something else.

It has been quite humiliating for me to find out (from Graves and Hodge) that my bad habits are the same as those of every other second rate writer outside the monastery. The same haste, distraction, etc. You very charitably put it down to a supernatural attitude on my part. Yes and no. It is true that when I drop the work and go to do something else I try not to think any more about it, and to be busy with the things that are really supposed to preoccupy a contemplative. When I succeed it means that I only think about the book in hand for two hours a day and that means a lot of loose thinking that goes through the machine and comes out on paper in something of a mess. And consequently I have to admit that much of the *Mountain* is pure first draught writing with nothing added except a few commas. That accounts for the heaviness of the long section preceding my Baptism—in which I think the cuts should come more than anywhere else. On the whole I think my haste is just as immoral as anybody else's and comes from the same selfish desire to get quick results with a small amount of effort. In the end, the whole question is largely an ascetic one! And incidentally I would never reproach anyone like yourself with vanity for wanting to write really well! I wish I had some of your integrity.

Really I like *The Reader Over Your Shoulder* very much. In the first place it is amusing. And I like their thesis that we are heading towards a clean, clear kind of prose. Really everything in my nature—and in my vocation too— demands something like that if I am to go on writing. The contemplative life demands that everything, all ones *[sic]* habits of thought and modes of action should be simple and definite and free of waste motion. In every department of our life that is our biggest struggle. You would be shocked to know how much material and spiritual junk can accumulate in the corners of a monastery and in the minds of the monks. You ought to see the pigsty in which I am writing this letter. There are two big crates of some unidentified printed work the monastery wants to sell. About a thousand odd copies of ancient magazines that ought to have been sent to the Little Sisters of the Poor, a dozen atrocious looking armchairs and piano stools that are used in the sanctuary for Pontifical Masses and stored on the back of my neck the rest of the time. Finally I am myself embedded in a small skyscraper of mixed books and magazines in which all kinds of surreal stuff is sitting on top of theology. All this is dominated by a big movie-star statue of Our Lady life-size, on a pedestal, taking up most of the room; it was spirited out of the lay brothers' choir when they varnished the floor of the church last spring, and never found its way back

Before I get into any more digressions I want to thank you for your offer to edit the English edition of the *Mountain*. The letter just came from Hollis and Carter and I gladly accept your offer. I was thinking that, for my own part, I could go over the book and make the corrections that occur to me and then send it along to you, to work with. As for the Cambridge business I will rewrite the whole thing if you wish. I would gladly see the whole tone of that passage changed. I am glad the book will be shorter.

I am sorry to think that I gave the impression I was looking down my nose at the Franciscans and I hope their feelings won't be hurt. They were very nice to me. However, about the love affairs I am afraid nothing more than what is there will get past a religious censor and there is nothing that can be done about it. I had to practically move a mountain to get across that passage where Peggy Wells came back and spent the night in the same room as Gibney and myself—and only did so by juggling it around and trying to disguise the fact that it was only a one room apartment.[18]

I am sending you a book of poems I wrote although I am ashamed of it. If you have any good ideas about them, let me know. I have practically stopped writing verse for the moment. I also sent you a pamphlet about the monastery and extracts from a magazine article in the official publication of the Order. You will find a lot of misprints made by the Belgian typesetters. Perhaps the subject matter is too technical to be really interesting but I thought you might get something out of it.

Since I last wrote to you our Abbot died[19] and we have a new one who just flew away to go to the General Chapter in France. He is a very holy man and he will be glad if I extricate myself from the network of trivialities into which the magazines are trying to get me. The Vicar General of the Order[20] came from France and I talked with him a lot, being his interpreter in the regular visitation of the house, and he had a lot of ideas that harmonized with yours, so definitely I shall try to keep out of useless small projects that do nothing but cause a distraction and dilute the quality of what I turn out. The big trouble is that in those two hours a day when I get at a typewriter I am always having to do odd jobs and errands and I am getting a lot of letters from strangers too. These I hope to take care of with a printed slip telling them politely to lay off the poor monk, let the guy pray.

Hollis and Carter may want the next book I am doing for Harcourt Brace, which is about the Order and our life.[21] Will it be all right if we shoot the proofs along to you when they come out, next spring or early summer? God forbid that I should impose on your kindness, so if you cannot read it please say so. But since you might be interested I thought I would mention it, anyway. Meanwhile I am waiting to get busy on the manuscript again.

I don't agree with Mgr. Knox[22] that God isn't interested in good prose. True, it doesn't mean anything to Him *per se,* and St. Paul seems to be on Mgr. Knox's side of the argument. But I don't think that Our Lord is very pleased with preachers and writers who do their best to get the Church all mixed up. Then there is that line about the judgement meted out for every idle word. It makes me very happy to think that you are going to judge the idle words in *The Seven Storey Mountain* before God does.

Meanwhile I pray for you, and please do you also pray for me. Don't be afraid to have a great devotion to Our Lady and say the Rosary a lot. Do you have any time for mental prayer? You have the gifts that grace works on and if you are not something of a contemplative already, you should be. Tell me to mind my own business—but in a way, it is my business. Anyway, God bless you, and thank you very much.

In Corde Christi,
Frater M. Louis O.C.R.

PS A Carthusian I write to at Parkminster[23] tells me they want to print something here to arouse at least a remote interest in a possible foundation in the U.S. If you have any connections here that would be interested in such a thing you might let me discreetly know—but discreetly. And I would pass the information on to the Carthusians.

Waugh's reply to that letter has been lost. Merton's return letter is almost devoid of writing-related content. Instead, the roles of master and student are switched and Merton becomes Waugh's spiritual director. From the monk's response, with his use of the second person singular in nearly every sentence ("your contrition," "all you need"), hortatory turn of phrase ("you ought to do so"), and direct references to Waugh's letter ("in all your anxiety to explain how your contrition is imperfect"), it is clear that the novelist had revealed something of his own spiritual malaise. The list of his spiritual woes was long—

the lack of any feeling of love toward his own children, his indifference to others and tendency toward cruelty, his remorse at feeling no guilt, his lack of sorrow over his failings, his inability to pray with any conviction—and this new correspondent, who spent his days in silence and prayer, was an obvious Father Confessor in whom Waugh could confide some of his troubles.

Dear Mr. Waugh,

I am very glad you went ahead with the editing of the Seven Storey Molehill. Since you have probably cut more than I would have, it will save me useless labor. I'll wait for the proofs and then catch the one or two lines you may have missed. I don't expect to have to add anything—I mean restore anything—unless you have cut out the fact that I was baptized and became a monk. All the rest is accidental.

Your last paragraph interested me much. Like all people with intellectual gifts, you would like to argue yourself into a quandary that doesn't exist. Don't you see that in all your anxiety to explain how your contrition is imperfect you are expressing an instant sorrow that it is *not* so—and that is true contrition. After all if you are sorry because your sorrow is not sorrowful because of God, then you *are* sorrowful because of God, not because of yourself. Two negatives make an affirmative. All you need is to stop speculating about it, and somewhere around the second step of your analysis, make a definite act of will, and rest in that. Then you will be practising a whole lot of supernatural virtues—above all, trust (hope). The virtue of hope is the one talented people most need. They tend to trust in themselves—and when their own resources fail then they will prefer despair to reliance on anyone else, even on God. It gives them a kind of feeling of distinction.

Really I think it might do you a lot of good and give you a certain happiness to say the Rosary every day. If you don't like it, so much the better, because then you would deliver yourself from the servitude of doing things for your own satisfaction: and that slavery to our own desires is a terrific burden. I mean if you could do it as a more or less blind act of love and homage to Our Lady, not bothering to try and find out where the attraction of the thing could possibly be hidden and why other people seem to like it. The real motive for this devotion at the moment is that the Church is very explicit: a tremendous amount depends on the Rosary and *everything* depends on Our Lady. Still, if there is some reasonable difficulty I don't know about, don't feel that you *have* to try this just because someone suggests it!

But things are so serious now—and values are so completely cockeyed—that it seems to me a matter of the highest moment to get even one individual to make one more act of his free will, directing it to God in love and faith. Everything—the whole history of our world—is hanging on such acts. Have you read St. John of the Cross? You ought to do so—he is terrific and also he is very *clear*, in spite of what people say about his difficulty.

I envy you your leisure. I would be sitting on top of the Cotswolds all day long in a trance. If you don't say many rosaries at least please some time say one for me. I am haunted by two ideas: solitude & poverty. I pray for you a lot, especially at Communion, & for your family. Someone told me you are doing a feature for *Life* on the Church in America. We *think* we are much better than we are. We have a big showy front. Behind it—there is a lot of good will that loses itself in useless activity and human ambition and display.

In Corde Jesu,
Fr. M. Louis O.C.R.

PS Once again—I am tremendously grateful for your kindness in editing that book for me. God bless you for it.

3

"Very nice and friendly"

NOVEMBER 1948

Vague plans for Waugh's second trip to the United States had been mooted for some time, even before he had known of Merton's existence. In 1947 he had received a letter from Father Francis X. Talbot, the Jesuit president of Loyola University in Baltimore, telling him that the university was conferring an honorary doctorate on him. Although he had the page proofs of *Brideshead Revisited* bound into a book as a thank-you gift for the university, he wrote to a friend that Loyola University was "not an illustrious seat of learning."[24] When Father Talbot further suggested that he undertake a lecture tour of American Catholic universities, however, the idea began to appeal to him. It would be an escape from dreary postwar Britain, and the proposed trip would allow him to visit some of the cities in the eastern United States, which he had not had a chance to see on the earlier trip. And finally, in the summer of 1948—having just read *The Seven Storey Mountain*—he was gripped by the prospect of writing an article for *Life* on American Catholicism.

The article proposal was unusual for the late 1940s: Catholics were still an immigrant group in the United States, the majority of them living in lower-middle-class ghettos, a far cry from places of power and from Waugh's own privileged life and his experience of the Catholic Church. In a letter to *Life*'s managing editor, John Shaw Billings, he alluded to an attitude of the American Catholic clergy that seemed broader than what he had encountered in England, especially with regard to immigrant communities, and this intrigued him. He also pointed out that he was particularly interested in American monasticism because of the recent book written by the young Trappist monk Thomas Merton.

As Waugh's ambition for the project grew, the American visit expanded into two trips. The first one, in the late months of 1948, would be a research trip, and the second, in the early months of 1949, would be a lecture tour. There remained the question of funding. Waugh wanted more than comfort during his travels; he wanted luxury—more than the Jesuits, or any university, could afford. Through his American agent he negotiated with *Life* a relatively modest fee for the article, $1000, and an extravagant $4000 for travel expenses.

He set sail for New York on the *Queen Elizabeth* on October 31, seeking religious enlightenment and spiritual renewal in the country he had, a year earlier, disparaged.

The financial terms he had negotiated, however, ensured that Christian simplicity and hard-rock asceticism were not part of the agreement. He arrived at New York harbor in a doleful mood, afflicted with a painful boil, and his first days were spent with the ministrations of various doctors. But the mahogany furnishings and the marble and gilt of the Plaza Hotel, where he stayed, pleased him. He found the powerful Luces to be incompatible companions—he, dreadfully stupid; she, self-centered and boring—but he soldiered through their hospitality, enjoying the caviar, champagne, and brandy they provided. He was entertained at high-class clubs, cocktail parties, and fashionable luncheons, and had reunions with his friends Oswald and Edith Sitwell and Maurice Bowra. He wrote details of the social whirlwind to his wife, and ended one letter with a rueful comment: "You will think all this time has not been spent much in Catholic enquiries & you will be right really."[25]

In the midst of the glitter and New York partying was another visit: to the social activist Dorothy Day (another Catholic convert), who was one of the founders of the Catholic Worker Movement. Dorothy Day lived on Mott Street in the Lower East Side of Manhattan and ran a soup kitchen there. Her name was on a list of people Waugh's Jesuit friend and spiritual guide, Martin D'Arcy, had given him. The bread line was forming for the noon meal as Waugh's car, a Cadillac, pulled up at the Catholic

Worker's House of Hospitality. He immediately earned Day's disapproval by suggesting he take her and her staff to lunch at Le Chambord, one of the most expensive restaurants in the city. She suggested a compromise in the form of an Italian restaurant in the neighborhood, where they spent several hours talking. The staff—to her further disapproval—accepted Waugh's offer of cocktails and wine. Characteristically, in his letter home Waugh said little about the spiritual impact of the Catholic Worker experience on him, except for an acerbic description of Day as "an autocratic ascetic saint."[26]

A modest itinerary to other cities had been planned for him, taking him to Boston, Baltimore, and Cincinnati, where, as a rather dumpy figure in a three-piece pinstripe suit and bow tie, he was introduced to the members of one club after another. Most of these he found boring, the clubs full of tedious talk and inedible food and heavily weighted with numbing historical importance. While giving a talk to a creative writing class at the Jesuit-run Boston College, Waugh revealed his own writing method: that he usually wrote two complete drafts of a manuscript before sending it for publication, that he preferred writing in longhand to using a typewriter because it gave him greater freedom to revise, and that he wrote chapter after chapter without planning his books in advance. But for Waugh, such side trips produced only melancholy and added to the realization that this journey was giving him very little experience of the Catholic Church in America.

He had, however, named one particular person whom he wanted to meet on this American journey: the Trappist Thomas Merton. He left Cincinnati for Louisville, Kentucky, on November 27, and from there he was driven to Gethsemani Abbey.

For Merton, the first hint that Evelyn Waugh was in America and planning to visit Gethsemani came in a flurry of telephone calls from *Time* magazine and telegrams from the publisher Harcourt Brace. He recorded this news in his journal on November 14. Neither telephone calls nor telegrams indicated when Waugh would arrive. When the novelist finally passed under Gethsemani's gatehouse archway and glimpsed its inlaid Latin greeting *Pax Intrantibus* ("Peace to those who enter"), most of the rambling monastery was in darkness. The monks had retired at 7:00 PM.

It is unlikely that Waugh attended Gethsemani's 3:00 AM monastic prayer known as Matins and Lauds, and so his first sighting of the monks would have been at the 7:45 AM High Mass on Sunday, November 28, in the Gothic simplicity of the abbey church, where he saw from a distance the row upon row of white-robed figures, many of them young, and almost a third novices. Brother Louis, the monk he had come to visit, was not distinguishable from any of the others. Waugh, who loved the ordered ritual of Mass, cannot but have been moved by the monastic ceremony: the reverent bowing and slow movements of the priest, the deacon, subdeacon, and acolytes, each having a role to play in the liturgical celebration, all to the sound of Gregorian chant sung by the choir monks.

Shortly after the conclusion of Mass, the two writers met in the visitors' parlor, where straight-backed chairs were the only furnishings. Both were mildly surprised, having had different expectations of the other's physical appearance. Waugh expected the tonsured, habited Merton to be older, but he found the monk humble and unspoiled by his newfound worldly success. His humorous and slangy speech left the novelist in little doubt that in different dress Merton would have fit easily into the bohemian world of New York's Greenwich Village.

Merton's journal account three days afterward summarizes the encounter, without further comment. "I expected him [Waugh] to be taller and more dashing," Merton writes, "but he was very nice and friendly."[27] Among famous writers' descriptions of other famous writers, "very nice and friendly" ranks as one of the most bland and colorless set of words, with the added irony that when one thinks about Evelyn Waugh's reputation as a human being, "very nice and friendly" is not the phrase that springs to mind.

There was probably an element of shyness on the part of both of them during that encounter. The austerity of Trappists was legendary. They slept in their religious habits and rose from beds consisting of straw-covered boards at 2:00 AM; spent more than seven hours a day in prayer; did heavy manual work; and ate sparingly with no meat and, during their long fasts, which lasted about half the year, no eggs or dairy products. Apart from their time in choir, they spent their days in silence, with no recreation.

Kneeling in the stark abbey church dressed in his tailor-made three-piece suit, fresh from the worldly elegance of high-society parties featuring caviar and fine wines, Waugh saw a monastic choir bursting with young monks who were embracing a life of contemplation and sacrifice. He himself was at the peak of his writing career at this time, but as a serious Christian he was all too aware of his personal shortcomings and found prayer to be an exercise in frustration. One can only conjecture that it was a humbling experience for him to see the monks file out in silence from the Gethsemani church and then to meet face-to-face the one he had come to see: the man who had lived a smart, sophisticated, youthful life similar to his own and had given it all up.

For Merton's part, he was in awe at Evelyn Waugh as a writer. As a student at Columbia University, Merton had been part of a cutting-edge artistic crowd with serious literary ambitions. His zealous postconversion desire to forego these ambitions had been thwarted by both his abbot's wishes and his own creative impulses. The success of *The Seven Storey Mountain* had exceeded all expectations, but he was aware of the imperfections in his own work. One of the best writers of English prose had pointed out the errors in style that he himself should have been aware of, and thus his cockiness as a writer had been brought down somewhat. By instinct he wanted to write well. It was humiliating to think of his writing as second-rate. He possibly felt, then, somewhat intimidated in meeting the great master of the English novel.

According to Merton's journal the first thing Waugh did upon their meeting was to chastise him for the suffocating heat of the monastery. Merton had declared in *The Seven Storey Mountain* that its rooms were freezing, Waugh pointed out, and therefore his claim in the book was exaggerated. The monk explained that there was a boiler problem, but Waugh appeared to be unconvinced. It was not unusual for Waugh to initiate an encounter with a complaint, whether real or feigned, and the heat comment indicates that they established an easy rapport. From Merton's journal account and a recollection nearly twenty years later,[28] it was a pleasant conversation between two sophisticated and worldly wise men who appreciated each other's inherent iconoclasm and sense of irony. Waugh spoke of drunken escapades and told Merton about his previous year's trip to Hollywood, which he had found boring. The movie capital, he said, far from containing the trappings of exoticism, consisted of business-suited men going about their work. The only entertainment was in the Los Angeles cemetery, which he visited every day. He also said he was "doing America the way Americans do Europe," visiting a city a day. On that topic he told Merton that he had "energetically" refused the hospitality of the archbishop of New Orleans, a comment that was sure to amuse the iconoclast in Merton. They spoke about church art and architecture and about poetry, Waugh saying that he could not read any poetry since Tennyson. His reaction to the book of Merton's own poetry the monk had sent him is unrecorded.

Waugh told Merton about his main project for this American trip: his article for *Life* magazine on the Catholic Church in America. This was another reason for Waugh to feel shy about a topic that was over his head. Merton writes, "he kept repeating that it would 'necessarily be superficial.' He is very careful about trying to do things well, if possible, and so he wants to prepare everyone in case this cannot be done marvellously well."[29]

In the context of Waugh's purported reason for the American trip—to learn about American Catholicism so as to write about it, and in particular his enthusiasm for

American monasticism—to what extent did he actually quiz Merton on the nuts and bolts of the monastic life? There is no indication that he showed any curiosity about the spiritual lives of the monks. His sharp eye may have observed the monk-author's restlessness, his unease with recent fame and the narcissism that accompanied it. (Merton had already been wrestling with a vision of the popular movie actor Gary Cooper playing the lead role in the film version of the book.)

In his letter to Waugh of September 22, 1948, Merton had mentioned a preoccupation with solitude ("I am haunted by two ideas: solitude and poverty"), and in subsequent letters, he refers to his own dissatisfaction with the barnacles of monastic life and the noisy machines outside his work area. He had, by this time, already been seeking long stretches of time for meditation in the woods and meadows and had thoughts of leaving the Trappists to join the Carthusians, a religious order with even more silence and more periods of prayer. These references in his letters and allusions to the Carthusians in their later exchanges suggest that Merton spoke to Waugh of his monastic frustrations during the morning's encounter. Sitting across from Merton in the monastery parlor—a close-up view, as it were, of a real Trappist monk who conversed with lively humor in American slang—Waugh may have already felt a dimming of the religious glow that had so captured his imagination upon his reading of the younger man's life story.

As for Merton, if he sensed a yearning spirit filled with self-disgust lurking behind the novelist's dark humor and the cosmopolitan camaraderie, he does not mention it. They parted on friendly terms, with Merton expressing the hope that Waugh would return to Gethsemani for a longer period, and Waugh warmly agreeing. Waugh left at noon, disappearing into a Kentucky rainstorm. He had spent less than twenty-four hours at an American Catholic monastery.

From Gethsemani Waugh moved on to New Orleans. He stayed at a hotel in the Garden District, where once again he complained of the heat and threatened to break a window unless the management opened it. As a result of the rumpus that resulted, he was asked to leave, and he ended his stay in the Roosevelt Hotel. In this city he saw French Catholic and Creole traditions mixed together in churches filled with statuary, icons, candles, and flowers, and he noticed African American people of all ages kneeling in devotion.

By the first week of December he was back in New York and eagerly welcomed a visit to Princeton University in New Jersey, where the eminent French Thomistic philosopher Jacques Maritain was on the faculty. The meeting of the two famous Catholic converts was not a success, the conversation veering too close to politics. Maritain's tendency was toward the left (he described himself as a "revolutionary"), and he was not always in sync with popular Catholic causes. Sharp disagreement on the Spanish Civil War and the papal social encyclicals reflected their different approaches to Catholicism. Perhaps as well their personalities and backgrounds were too dissimilar for a satisfying meeting of minds to take place.

Waugh set sail on his return to England on December 22. As he was approaching the ship, a young woman, who turned out to be a newspaper reporter, approached him. What impressed him most in the United States? the reporter wanted to know. "The Trappist monastery in Kentucky," he replied, and he proceeded to fill her in on matters concerning monasticism. Obviously less than interested in such concerns, she regaled her readers with Waugh's further impressions: that American rooms were too hot, that windows were nailed down and could not be opened, that Americans chewed colored bubble gum, and that they kept radios on all day and talked too much. . . .

4

Elected Silence

*T*he *Seven Storey Mountain* made its first appearance on the bestseller nonfiction list just before Christmas of 1948, appearing as number sixteen. It was to remain on the bestseller list for sixty-two consecutive weeks, hovering between number two and number three for the following year.

In the meantime, as the calendar turned over into January 1949, Evelyn Waugh prepared for his lecture tour of the United States, and the galley proofs of the British edition of *The Seven Storey Mountain* were completed. When the proofs reached Merton early in the new year, he discovered that the title had been changed to *Elected Silence*. These were the first two words of a poem called "The Habit of Perfection" by Gerard Manley Hopkins, who had died in 1889 and whose collection of poems was published only in 1918. The poem praises the silence that is "elected," or chosen, in the life of one who has given oneself completely to God. (Despite Waugh's claim that he read no poetry after Tennyson, he had already given his novel *A Handful of Dust* a title from an even more recent poem, T. S. Eliot's *The Waste Land*.)

The new title of Merton's work represented Waugh's preference for clarity over abstruseness. Although most of the book is taken up with Merton's premonastic life, much of it the antithesis of silence, the change of title for British readers offers a hint of Waugh's altered emphasis. If Merton minded the change from the penitential climb implied in *The Seven Storey Mountain*'s title, there is no indication of this.

Waugh's approach to writing was that of a craftsman, and he was meticulous in putting words together to form a sentence. He considered writing to be an exacting practice rather than a slapdash one, and he expected the same care to be taken by other writers. Merton was a fast writer. His approach, given his limited amount of writing time, was to tap out whatever came into his mind, perhaps trying various ways of saying the same thing in order to make a point. Editing was a luxury he had no time for. When one examines the pages of *The Seven Storey Mountain*, as Waugh the editor did, this free-fall style is all too evident. It is a credit to Merton's ability as a writer that the prose is as lucid and beautiful as it is. In the interest of having his author say everything only once, however, Waugh cut through many paragraphs such as the following, which has to do with Merton's master's thesis, "Nature and Art in William Blake" (the excised parts are in italics):

> What it amounted to, was a study of Blake's reaction against every kind of literalism and naturalism and narrow, classical realism art, because of his own ideal which was essentially mystical and supernatural. *In other words, the topic, if I treated it at all sensibly, could not help but cure me of all the naturalism and materialism in my own philosophy.*
>
> . . .
>
> *. . . It produced a kind of intuitive perception of reality through a sort of affective identification with the object contemplated—the kind of perception that the Thomists call "connatural." This means . . .*[30] [and so he goes on for three more paragraphs, all of which Waugh cut].

The phrase *In other words* and the lead-in words *This means* were red flags for Waugh; they signaled either a repetition of something already said immediately before or an explanation that threatened to interrupt the account of the author's life.

Waugh regarded *The Seven Storey Mountain* essentially as a story, and therefore he strove to cast aside anything that impeded the narrative flow. Stories work best when they put people, or characters, at the center, rather than abstract ideas or the musings that follow rhetorical questions. And thus the reason for Waugh's removal of the extraneous bits from the following:

> Now my life was dominated by something I had never really known before: fear. *Was it really something altogether new? No, for fear is inseparable from pride and lust. They may hide it for a time; but it is the reverse of the coin.*[31]

Note the rhetorical question and the digression that flows from it.

This example also highlights another category of material that Waugh took out—excessive self-castigation. *The Seven Storey Mountain* has plenty of this, beginning with the young child whose mother is dying. The following sentences come right after the paragraph in which six-year-old Tom reads the note his mother has written to him from the hospital, telling him that she will never see him again.

> *Prayer? No, prayer did not even occur to me. How fantastic that will seem to a Catholic—that a six-year-old child should find out that his mother is dying and not know enough to pray for her!* It was not until I became a Catholic, twenty years later, that it finally occurred to me to pray for my mother.[32]

Merton is so hard on his childhood self in those two sentences that it seems almost an act of mercy for Waugh to have excised them.

A whole paragraph, coming soon after the description of Merton's baptism, also got the chop:

> *The only thing that saved me was my ignorance. Because in actual fact, since my life after my Baptism was pretty much what it had been before Baptism, I was in the condition of those who despise God by loving the world and their own flesh rather than Him.*[33]

"Because"—another word signaling overexplanation. Other red flags appeared in the form of words that prefaced speculation, most of which Waugh considered to be useless—such as "perhaps" or the verb phrase "must have," as in the following, which comes immediately after the death of Merton's mother:

> When we got home to Douglaston, Father went into a room alone, and I followed him and found him weeping, over by the window. *He must have thought of the days before the war, when he had first met mother in Paris.*[34]

What exactly his father thought at that moment was, of course, not known, and so Waugh considered it superfluous.

He may also have regarded it as a sentimental frill added onto a picture of grief that speaks for itself.

Waugh cut whole swathes of unnecessary piety, not only because it impeded the flow of the story, but also because Merton, with his convert's zeal, tended to crow with insistent triumphalism in some passages about the superiority of Catholicism and its doctrinal and moral purity. Waugh was equally rigid in his belief, yet practiced his Catholicism within a diverse milieu, and he excised such judgmental and demeaning comments as "he detested Catholics, like most Protestant ministers."[35] Paragraphs describing Merton's bitterness toward Cambridge were taken out for the reason, as Waugh had explained in his first letter to Merton, that he thought the fault lay more with the young man's own recklessness as a student rather than with Cambridge University itself.

Waugh also saw passages where excess wording clouded over the emotional intensity of a situation. Paring away the verbal fat highlighted the emotion. One such bloated section comes at the end of part 1, where, with the extraneous bits removed, the paragraph ends with a stark declarative sentence.

Such was the death of the hero, the great man I had wanted to be. *Externally (I thought) I was a big success. Everybody knew who I was at Columbia.*

. . . And yet I know how capable they were of say-
ing many words, not tastefully chosen, perhaps, but
deadly enough.
The wounds within me were, I suppose, enough.[36]

Waugh wrote the foreword to *Elected Silence*, telling
readers that the text had been "very slightly abridged"[37]
in order that it might appeal to European taste. He
said that nothing had been omitted except for passages
"which seemed to be of purely local interest" (a generous
statement). Thus, much about his father (whom Waugh
obviously considered to be of less importance to Merton's
story than Merton himself did) was omitted from the
British edition, as were such Columbia University people
as Merton's mentor, Mark Van Doren.

Waugh's editing technique was to cut rather than
to rewrite. Nothing, in fact, was rewritten in the British
version of the book, and thus Merton's distinct voice
remains, with few exceptions. One such exception appears
in the editing of the sentence "I had a date with someone
with whom I liked very much to have a date."[38] This is
a brash sentence, indicating a young man's bravado—an
empty bravado, as it turns out—but that is part of the
attractiveness of Merton's writing style: cocky and at the
same time self-aware. For Waugh, this sentence contained
a redundancy, and he changed it to "I had a date with

someone whom I liked very much,"[39] thus turning it into a bland, prim sentence that anyone could have written. The shortened version also contains a shift in nuance: did Merton actually like the "someone" in question, or did he simply like having a date with her? This was a rare misstep for Waugh the editor. Another was the excision of the two poems that had made their way into *The Seven Storey Mountain*. The removal of "Our Lady of Cobra," in the section on Cuba, may not have been missed, but millions of readers over the years have been emotionally moved by the eloquent addition of "For My Brother: Reported Missing in Action, 1943," at the end of the section describing his brother John Paul's death. But due to Waugh's editing out of the two poems, the British readers of the book did not have the chance to be so moved.

At any rate, Merton professed himself delighted with the master's editing job, and there is no indication anywhere in his journal to suggest that he was anything but grateful. *Elected Silence* reached the British public soon into the new year of 1949 to appreciative reviews. (Later in the year the critic V. S. Pritchett would write a skeptical review of the book, and in response Waugh wrote that Pritchett "admits that he has so far forgotten what he was taught, that 'the existence of God, the truth of the Bible, the reality of prayer' are meaningless phrases to him. He does not know whether Vocation exists. Yet he does not feel any doubt about his competence to review a book on the subject. Try him on Mathematics. I am sure a lot of American books on that subject get overpraised."[40]) The first printing of the book sold out immediately. By the end of January Waugh was already back in the United States, accompanied by his wife, Laura, and wearing a heavy houndstooth coat and bowler hat. He was all set to begin his lecture tour and soak up more of American Catholicism.

Dear Mr. Waugh: FEBRUARY 19, 1949

As far as I can judge, you must be back in America at the moment, finishing your articles for *Life*. So I am writing to you in New York, first of all to thank you for the preface to *Elected Silence*, a copy of which was sent to me, and which was very kind indeed, and second to assure you that the edition of *E.S.* by you is much less cut than I expected. I have not gone through it all, since Hollis and Carter said they would not have time to incorporate any corrections I might make in their edition anyway, but from what I have seen, the book is improved considerably.

I hope we are going to see those articles—and I hope you have not said anything too flattering about American Catholics. There is a fair amount of ferment, I suppose, in the church, but I wonder how deep it goes in this country. We still need an interior life—and a few sacrifices. On the other hand I am constantly impressed by the amount of good theological writing that is coming out of France, especially from the Editions du Cerf.

New Directions is putting out a book I wrote and which purports to be spiritual.[41] There is a deluxe edition of the thing, on special paper and in a box. When I was signing the colophon sheets, I reflected on the nature of the work itself and began to feel very foolish. As I progressed I was tempted to write flippant and even obscene remarks over the signature, so perhaps the whole scheme did not come from the Holy Ghost. But in any case I'll send you a copy of this book in its dressed up edition. It is beautifully printed.

Speaking of New Directions, I told Laughlin you said you had met him and he became very agitated and made me promise to inform you that the man from New Directions whom you met was not Laughlin but one of his henchmen, a Tony Bower with whom he does not wish to be confused because he is "a character." Anyway, it was not you who told me you had met Laughlin, but I insisted that it was Laughlin you had met when you said you had had lunch with someone from New Directions. There, I hope that is settled.

Don't forget, please, that we extorted a promise that you would come back here some time. God bless you. Say some Rosaries too, if Our Lady inspires you, it is very healthy.

In Corde Christi,
Fr. M. Louis o.c.r.

5

"The American epoch"

MARCH–SEPTEMBER 1949

Waugh, accompanied by his wife, arrived back in the United States on January 24, 1949. His lecture tour, lasting six weeks and arranged mainly for Catholic colleges, covered an area between Boston and New Orleans. The plan was to spend three days in each place to give Waugh a chance to meet students, college faculty, and clergy. Travel was by first-class rail, and the Waughs were to stay in the best hotels, the cost covered by the agreement with *Life*. The lecture topic at each college was a variation of Waugh's critical study of three English Catholic convert writers: G. K. Chesterton, Ronald Knox, and Graham Greene, the latter two of whom were his personal friends.

Described by a *Washington Post* journalist as "short, bland, double-chinned and endowed with a dolefully suspicious glance,"[42] Waugh stood out everywhere with his long, heavy tweed coat, bowler hat, and walking stick. In the lecture halls he dazzled the audiences, speaking without notes. Outside he was sometimes rude toward his hosts—a tendency, accepted by his friends, that shocked and bewildered those who did not know him—but at other times he appeared gracious and "unremittingly decent."[43] Both sides of the novelist appeared in Mobile, Alabama: according to an account written later by his host, the Jesuit J. Franklin Murray, Waugh was taken to the city's top attraction, an estate filled with a series of landscaped flower gardens and pathways, called Bellingrath Gardens. Spotting a "Keep Off the Grass" sign, he dropped to his hands and knees, pulled up some of the grass, and scattered it, declaring his own garden in England to be superior. Later the same day "the better Waugh came out"[44] when he met a group of Jesuit seminarians and offered critical remarks about *Brideshead Revisited* and about English Jesuit writers he admired. He was seen to drink vast amounts of alcohol throughout the tour, despite the restrictive laws in some states; according to Father Murray's account, at a dinner before his Mobile lecture, he consumed two cocktails, two bottles of burgundy, and a glass of brandy, all the while becoming tipsily animated. By the time he reached the podium a few moments later, however, he appeared sober and delivered a brilliant lecture.

After his talk at Notre Dame University, near South Bend, Indiana, Waugh was accompanied by a student reporter on his way through pouring rain to the train station. What did he think of America? the student wanted to know. Although Waugh would later write that he was impressed with the Notre Dame students' devotion in the chapel, he chose to give the student a more down-to-earth response, and the university newspaper gave the gist of it, to the probable delight of the student body: "I should think you would have huge tankards of wine and liquor at the end of your [cafeteria] lines instead of those teetotalling liquids. One should consume great quantities of wine while eating."[45] As he boarded the train to leave, holding up a black umbrella against the rain, he recited the first verse of G. K. Chesterton's poem "The Song of Right and Wrong," on the benefits of alcohol:

Feast on wine or fast on water
And your honour shall stand sure,
God almighty's son and daughter
He the valiant, she the pure;
If an angel out of heaven
Brings you other things to drink,
Thank him for his kind attention.
Go and pour them down the sink.

In St. Paul he met the writer J. F. Powers, whose fictional stories about troubled priests Waugh admired. In an interview published in the *Minneapolis Morning Tribune* he named Powers, Thomas Merton, and Erle

Stanley Gardner as his favorite American writers. (He liked the action in the latter's detective novels.) At Marquette University in Milwaukee he met Sister Thérèse Lentfoehr, a poet with whom Merton corresponded. Sister Thérèse had begun collecting Merton's cast-off materials, including the original manuscript of *The Seven Storey Mountain*. Waugh expressed interest in seeing the full-length version, hoping that some of the colorful parts that had been censored by either the Trappist Order or Merton himself might be put back in. (This never happened.) In a mischievous acknowledgment of American Catholicism at its most vulgar, he bought at a church-goods store in Illinois some religious gadgets that were purported to make it easier to pray the Rosary. He distributed these to at least two of the Marquette lecture attendees, one of them Sister Thérèse, who described the object as "a 1 1/2 inch square plastic mechanism to carry in the pocket, with a clicking device which recorded the *Aves* and *Paters*."[46]

Waugh and his wife returned to England in mid-March, having left a string of both insults and pleasant encounters—and having provided for Father Murray the impetus for a "deep meditation about the value of hobnobbing with celebrities."[47]

~⌒⌐

Waugh wrote to Merton before returning to England, but the letter has not survived. At Gethsemani, Merton prepared for his ordination to the priesthood. The realization that he was becoming a monastic celebrity as a result of *The Seven Storey Mountain* was beginning to dawn on him as he tried to cope with the influx of mail from readers. He ruefully admitted in his journal that he had not foreseen fan mail as one of the crosses he would have to bear within the Trappist way of life. He also had several books at various stages of the publishing process, including *Seeds of Contemplation*, a series of reflections on the Christian spiritual life that presented an invitation to move, through contemplation, into an awareness and knowledge of God. (A sentence that seemed written almost specifically for Evelyn Waugh: "Prayer and love are learned in the hour when prayer has become impossible and your heart has turned to stone."[48])

Another one soon to be published was *The Waters of Siloe*, a history of the Cistercian Order in the United States. The title comes from Isaiah 8, referring to the water that gushed forth periodically into a stream, forming a pool in Jerusalem and becoming the site of one of Jesus's miracles (John 9). As Waugh was soon to find out, this book was dedicated to him.

Dear Mr. Waugh: MAY 12, 1949

Thank you very much for your last letter, written before you left New York. Since then a volume of *Seeds of Contemplation* has started on its way to Gloucestershire, where I hope it will find you well and happy and will not do anything to spoil your joy. I imagine you are quite relieved to be at home and in relative peace after your American campaign. Sister Thérèse, in Milwaukee and others here and there have written in to say that they succeeded in cornering you at odd moments on your lecture tour. Which brings to mind your kind offer to look at the original ms of *E. Silence* and perhaps incorporate unprinted passages in a second edition. I don't know if it would be worth the bother. Sister Thérèse, who is extremely kind-hearted, has a misguided notion that I am the cousin of Santa Claus and overestimates every word that I write by about seven hundred per cent. Perhaps it would be just as well to let it drop, although if you really *want* to undertake this penance, you may certainly have all the necessary permission.

I have taken the liberty of dedicating our book *Waters of Siloe* to you. I do hope you will not object to having your name appear in the front matter of the history of a religious Order—and a history which is not any too well written, either. But I wished to show you some exterior token of our gratitude and sincere friendship. Besides, I felt, quite selfishly, that the book would benefit by the presence of your name in it, and that this fact might even hoodwink some of the readers into thinking that the book had some merit.

I close assuring you that your account of the Chicago prayer-wheel, or the rosary-with-lights, has been haunting me for months.[49] No wonder Communism is so popular.

If you happen to be anywhere near here in two weeks, on Ascension day, or the two following, please consider yourself invited to my ordination and first low/then high Mass. In any case I know you will ask Our Lady to make me a simple and holy priest.

With all best wishes,
Sincerely in Corde Christi,
Fr. M. Louis O.C.R.

Merton's simple invitation to Waugh to attend his ordination to the priesthood belied the excitement he felt over the coming spiritual transformation in his life. He was ordained a deacon on March 17 and was overwhelmed and awed by the meaning reflected in that final step before priesthood. In the weeks that followed he was engrossed in the preparation for priestly ordination, learning the intricate rubrics of the liturgy and expending anxiety over the exact gestures, speech, and chant expected of ordained ministers during Mass. The ordination ceremony took place on May 26, and Merton celebrated his first Solemn High Mass two days later. The event marked an important new beginning for him, and he tried to size up his writing life in the context of his new priestly reality. (On the day of his ordination to the deaconate he had decided to give up writing poetry; as a result, he tore up some notes for poems, but as always, the decision did not stick for long.)

Waugh had been back in England for two months by this time, deeply depressed over the obligation now upon him to write an article for *Life* on American Catholicism. He told his friend Nancy Mitford that "there is nothing to say except that americans [*sic*] are louts & that Catholic Americans are just a little better than panglossist americans [*sic*]."[50] The grumbling masked his sense of inadequacy in the face of the task he had set himself and for which he found himself ill-prepared. He spent Holy Week and Easter at the Benedictine Abbey of Downside, which was his annual custom. A month later he managed to write a gracious letter to Merton on the occasion of the monk's priestly ordination. If he felt insulted by the dedication of a book whose writing Merton considered inferior, his letter gives no hint of it.

Dear Fr. Louis,   MAY 27 [1949]

First, my joy for you on your ordination. Your letter came just in time to engage my feeble prayers at the Ascension Day mass.

Secondly, my eager acceptance of the dedication of *Waters of Siloe*. It is an enormous honour I do not at all deserve.

Thirdly, my deep thanks for the beautiful copy of *Seeds of Contemplation*. . . .

I am struggling with the *Life* article on American Catholicism feeling daily more and more that it is an intolerably presumptuous undertaking.

. . . Another anecdote from the Springfield town-diocese shop. A traveler came with a new type of plastic crucifix and said, "Its great advantage is that it is so strong you can throw it on the ground and stamp on it. . . ."

. . . At Downside at Easter I had a long talk with a . . . Benedictine monk whose ambition for years has been to transfer to a Cistercian house. Permission for this transfer has now been finally refused at Rome. He had some knowledge of Parkminster and said that in his opinion the contemplative life was better lived among Cistercians than modern Carthusians whose solitude is constantly broken by bells calling them to mental prayer for specific objects. All these high matters are infinitely above me. I merely report what I am told. . . .

Please pray for me.

Yours very sincerely
Evelyn Waugh

In his letter, Waugh also tells Merton that he is sending him a book of sermons by his friend the priest and writer Ronald Knox. Knox, too, was a convert to Roman Catholicism. His father had been an Anglican bishop, and after succeeding brilliantly at Oxford University, he gave up a promising career by becoming a priest and was later named a monsignor. He had returned to Oxford as the Catholic chaplain, and by the late 1940s had embarked on his own translation of the Latin Vulgate Bible into English. To Waugh, Knox was the model of British Roman Catholicism, and his writing exemplified the best in spiritual prose. Although Waugh pointedly does not compare the two, Knox's writing was also more disciplined than Merton's.

In the meantime, Merton's work had been somewhat sidelined as he was given the task of writing the text for a book of photographs in preparation for the Abbey of Gethsemani's centenary. The celebration took place on June 1 with a solemn Mass in St. Mary's field, outside the monastery enclosure. Hundreds attended, a crew from Movietone News captured the event, and a radio interview was conducted with the famous monk-author, Thomas Merton.

A week later, the abbot general of the Cistercians arrived at the abbey. Merton discussed with him his desire for more solitude and his growing dissatisfaction with the businesslike atmosphere of Gethsemani, where work with machines was taking a central place, leaving monks with less and less time for reading and contemplation. Again, his desire to move elsewhere reared its head, and the question of a transfer to the Carthusians came up. And once again, his superiors vetoed any such move forward in that direction.

Dear Mr. Waugh,

Thank you for your letter of May 27th. I haven't seen any sign of the Ronald Knox book which you mentioned yet. Perhaps it got sidetracked somewhere in the Prior's shambles.

The Month[51] has been paying me for my effusions by sending me books. One of them was *The Loved One*. I was having a delightful time with it until the authorities discovered that it was a n-v-l and swept it away. I still have *Brideshead Revisited* here even though it is a n-v-l. (hush!) I am allowed it because it is a model for style. That was what I said, and it is absolutely true. It is beautifully done. The writing is so fine that I don't want to go on with the book at all, I just take a paragraph here and there and admire it, so that I haven't read *Brideshead* yet, either but have just enjoyed these fragments. I hope you are not offended.

Waters of Siloe, which is, on the other hand, a model of downright terrible writing, partly through my fault and partly through the fault of those through whose hands it passed on the way to the press, is now in print but not yet bound. Harcourt Brace will send you a copy as soon as possible, I hope. The date of publication is set for September 15th and there is already an enormous sale.

We had our centenary celebration. It only lasted one day. I learned later that one of the monks had thought up a horrible scheme for a three day celebration, the second day of which would feature a field Mass to be attended by twenty thousand school children. The archbishop nearly fainted when he heard of it. Fortunately it never went through. I was in charge of press-relations that day and sat in a press-box, no less, watching the field Mass as if it were a polo game. A week later someone called up on the telephone and by some mistake got me—I was the one he wanted anyway. His first question was "Do you have the rule of silence?" I said, "Who are *you,* anyway?" It turned out to be one of the reporters who had been here for the centenary. He was just trying to show off the fact that he now knew the difference between the rule of silence, which exists, and the vow of silence, which does not.

Since then it has been furiously hot here. Postulants keep arriving in great numbers and while we all sweat in the refectory a colored novice reads to us glowing accounts of how cold is the life of the missionaries among the Eskimos. It is a book which I find very thrilling although it contains horrible passages about people eating live fish and holding their mouths with their hands to keep the fish from jumping out while being chewed.

One of the postulants we have now wears a sport shirt that is covered with pictures of fox-hunting scenes dreamed up by some genius in the Seventh-Avenue ghetto of New York. Men on fat horses come whooping through the pack of hounds in every direction and I forget all about the psalms in my fascination at this curious piece of tapestry which is parked right in front of me.

If you want an idea for a novel I think I could start you on one, and find out the rest of the story. At four o'clock one morning a Negro in a dinner jacket showed up at the gate of a very prim Trappist monastery in France and said he had come all the way from Haiti to join. He was not wearing a dinner jacket because of dissipation, but because he believed one ought to dress as a waiter. He signed up in the book as the official guide to the cathedral in Port-au-Prince and became a monk but I have forgotten the funny details of his short stay in the monastery. He left the Trappists and went to the Dominicans in Angers and they did not let him become a novice but put him to work in the garden. There he found out that there was a very pretty maid who worked in one of the houses overlooking the garden and he fell madly in love with her, so that whenever she appeared at the windows he began throwing kisses to her. The story immediately got around Angers that the Dominicans were throwing kisses at all the maids in all the houses around their Friary and so the man was fired. I can find out about him and about the only American postulant who entered the same monastery. He became wildly incensed at the tyranny of the Trappist life and after a week in the monastery attacked the novice master with a pitchfork. He had previously rushed into the dormitory when nobody else was there and had scrawled "A Mort le Pere Maître" all over the cells with chalk.

The latest rumor about me is that I am in the Vatican studying ancient manuscripts about the Cistercian Order.[52] If you see me around London, let me know. Since Father Abbot lets me wander around in the woods by myself I am no longer so terribly bothered with the problem of solitude. Kentucky is mildly crazy but I suppose one can be a contemplative here as well as anywhere else in the world and the easy informality of monastic life in America is probably a great improvement over the tension which I suspect exists almost everywhere in Europe. A Chinese monk was here and he gave a graphic imitation of the French monks fighting in choir over details of the chant, in his Chinese monastery. Really I think you could write a wonderful novel about Trappists and it would give you an excuse to come and stay here for six months, in hiding. We would all be glad to have you. The Abbot General gave me a good story which I am going to use myself; it is the real account of what happened to one of our Brothers who was put in concentration camp by the Nazis and afterwards did some jobs for the French secret service and had some thrilling escapes from the Gestapo and whatnot. It sounds good.

There goes the bell. God bless you. I remember you at Mass and recommend you especially to Our Lady. Like everyone else in the world you are almost too shy about your religious possibilities.

In Corde Christi,
Fr. M. Louis O.C.R.

In Merton's talks with the abbot general, the questions about writing, solitude, and his continued monastic life had arisen. He was gratified to hear the abbot general not only say that his vocation remained as it already was—to continue writing—but also acknowledge Merton's need to be alone in the woods outside the monastic enclosure. Merton confided to his journal that meditation in the church was torturous and full of distractions, whereas praying in nature, among the trees and birds and other creatures of nature, directly under the sky, was peaceful and easy. Despite the gradual lifting of monastic strictures, however, he was also showing physical signs of tension and overwork; he fainted while trying to sing the Gospel at Mass one day, and stomach pains had surfaced as well.

As for Waugh, Merton was not the only young writer who was receiving the master's advice. Waugh had already suggested major changes to the structure of his good friend Nancy Mitford's latest manuscript, and when her novel appeared during the summer under the title *Love in a Cold Climate*, he was quick with praise.

His comments were more tart and bracing for George Orwell, his equal in stature and reputation. In Orwell's recently published *Nineteen Eighty-Four*, the author had made the Christian Church disappear, Waugh claimed in a letter to him, and as a result its absence left an improbable social and historical gap: even if conditions in 1984 turned out to be as Orwell showed in his book, he went on, there would still be clandestine Christians, and thus Christianity would continue to survive. (In all other respects Waugh admired Orwell, both as a writer and as a person.)

He had also been tracking the reviews of *Elected Silence*, and was gratified that British readers, fed on frivolous pictures of American life, were finally seeing, in the Trappist vocation, a side of the United States that was unknown to them. Then, in the late summer, fresh from Thomas Merton's American publisher, *The Waters of Siloe* arrived on his doorstep with the dedication: TO EVELYN WAUGH.

Dear Fr. Louis,

The Waters of Siloe arrived this morning. . . . I am proud to see my name on the fly-leaf. Thank you again for the dedication.

I have now finished *Seeds of Contemplation*. It is most kind and should do much [for] Catholics and heathen alike. I am impressed by your assurance. You write as if you had been a director of souls for a life time. Except perhaps that an experienced director would not, as you sometimes seem to do, press the need of contemplation on all so eagerly. Is it not rather a question of rate of growth. Of course the contemplative's ideal is what we must all come to before we reach heaven, and of course if one can, it is convenient to stop wasting time and get through as much as possible of purgation here. But don't you think most souls are of slow growth? . . . Is there not a slight hint of bustle and salesmanship about the way you want to scoop us all into a higher grade than we are fit for?

. . . *Elected Silence* has had a very respectful reception here—not particularly understanding in most cases, but it has been chosen by the magazines and papers as an important book. . . .

Yours ever
Evelyn Waugh

Waugh read the book immediately, while Merton, in his rural Kentucky monastery, found peace and a prayerful atmosphere among the horses in an old barn, and hoped (in vain, as it always happened) that he could put his writing and publishing on pause. Waugh wrote to him the day after he had received *The Waters of Siloe*.

Dear Fr. Louis,   AUGUST 29, 1949

I have now read *The Waters of Siloe* and I must write to repeat my thanks for the great honor you did me by dedicating it to me. Most of the subject matter was entirely new to me and I found it enthralling. . . .

May I, without presumption, make one or two technical criticisms of *The Waters of Siloe*. The arrangement seems to me a little loose. I do not see any need for the Prologue at all, which strikes the wrong artistic note, smacking of journalism in the way you try to catch the attention with an anecdote, and I don't really see that the Note on Contemplative Orders is required. Everything you say in it, is said better and more fully later on in the book. I have nothing but admiration for the narrative passages, except that there is no consistency of style. Sometimes you write literary English and sometimes slang.

And in the non-narrative passages, do you not think you tend to be diffuse, saying the same thing more than once. I noticed this in *The Seven Storey Mountain* and the fault persists. It is pattern-bombing instead of precision-bombing. You scatter a lot of missiles all round the target instead of concentrating on a single direct hit. It is not art. Your monastery tailor and boot-maker could not waste material. Words are our materials. . . .

Does it seem like looking a gift-horse in the teeth, to criticize like this? You must remember that you caused a great stir with your first book and it is the way of the world to watch enviously for signs of deterioration. I know you have no personal pride in your work, but you do not, I take it, want hostile critics to be able to say: "You see what religion has done for Merton. A promising man ruined by being turned on to make money for the monastery." . . .

Anyway they can't say it about this book which is full of vitality and interest. But I wish I saw the faults of *The Seven Storey Mountain* disappearing and I don't.

Yours ever,
Evelyn Waugh

In the letter, Waugh also suggests that Merton consider writing several volumes for popular readership on the history of Catholicism in America. He himself had looked for such a book, he added, when he was doing research for his *Life* article. Such volumes, he thought, would fill in the gaps left by Protestant histories. This was a strange suggestion for a strictly cloistered monk whose interests ran in the direction of monasticism, prayer, and contemplation, and it reflected, perhaps, Waugh's own paucity of knowledge in the field of American Catholicism's history. In his reply, Merton, whose life was already overcrowded, did not allude to the aberrant suggestion.

Dear Mr Waugh:

Thank you very much for your two letters and your very valuable advice on the two books, *Waters of Siloe* and *Seeds of Contemplation.* I heard indirectly from Hollis and Carter that you might let yourself be persuaded to edit *Waters* for the English public as you did the *Mountain.* I would never have dared to ask for such a favor but if there is any possibility of your doing it, I would be delighted at my good fortune.

Your comments on the structure of *Waters* are true. The book is now being read in the refectory and I am aware that the pattern bombing, as you call it, is even worse than in the *Mountain.* It would be a great deal tidier and better to get direct hits, as you say. Still, I know that in my spiritual reading, I am generally glad to find the same thing said over again three or four times and in three or four different ways. I think this is a characteristic of many people who try to say something about the spiritual life— not a virtue perhaps, but a characteristic fault. I am glad to have at least a fault in common with St. John of the Cross, but I agree that it would be better to get rid of it and acquire the virtue of precision instead. You know that slang is almost part of my nature. I shall, however, set myself to avoid it in at least one book, and see how it turns out. Recently, I went through a manuscript that I turned out when I thought I was being "disciplined" and the effect was horrible. It read like a literal translation from the German. My tendency is to tie myself up in knots when I get too self-conscious about what I am putting down on paper.

You console me greatly by objecting to the Prologue which I had thrown out and which the editor demanded back. The Note is my fault, and is a hypersensitive gesture of protection against critics who have been peppering me for my notions about the contemplative life.

Having found that even in a contemplative order men resent being hustled into contemplation (especially by one who is their junior in religion!!) I am pulling in my horns and will send you the article that results. One of the censors said it consoled him.

By the way, do not think that the faults of *Waters* are due to neglect of your advice about the *Mountain*. The book was finished long before the *Mountain* came out and I did not have a chance to do more than wipe out a few solecisms and make other corrections of that sort in proof. I should have caught more of the clichés. The trouble with writing here is that one has few contacts with healthy modern prose, and the things you hear in the refectory do not form your style! Then I have tended to rush too much. I have burned deep in my mind a statement from Graves and Hodge that faults of style are ultimately faults of character and have moral implications. Whatever happens, the next book will come out slowly and with thought and attention. I mean the next but one. The next is an atrocious life of a mediaeval stigmatic[53]—the one which I thought was disciplined, when I was writing it. Short of rewriting it I cannot seem to do anything about it. I ought to have the strength of character to refuse to let it be published at all.

In any case, I am glad to get such valuable and stimulating direction, and from one so marvellously qualified to give it. I have no difficulty in accepting you as the delegate of the Holy Ghost in this matter. By the way, I have been twisting and turning and trying to get Ward Fowler[54] from some source. Would you be annoyed if I finally turned and begged it from *you*? We have no copy in the house, and we do not have any decent (i.e. Oxford) dictionary here either. And I cap my insolence with the assurance that we would be delighted to get anything by Monsignor Knox.

In any case, God bless you. I keep you in my Mass every day and ask Our Lady to be with you and help you. Please pray for me too.

Yours in Corde Jesu Christi,
Fr. Louis O.C.R.

~ۑ

The book Merton requested from Waugh, Fowler's *Modern English Usage*, soon arrived, as did the September 19, 1949 issue of *Life*, containing Waugh's article "The American Epoch in the Catholic Church." The *Life* article, with photographs, covered twenty-one pages. It is a tribute to Waugh's stature as a writer, and perhaps to Clare Booth Luce's influence in the magazine (for surely it was she who persuaded her husband to have it printed), that such a lengthy and somewhat pedantic article took up so much space in a periodical that was essentially a popular picture magazine. In spite of Waugh's unease as he prepared the article, feeling he was not up to the job, his decades of journalistic observation and keenness for the Roman Catholic Church stood him in good stead. The article is in many ways a reflection on the manner in which the Catholic culture of postwar America was able to flourish within a country founded on Protestant principles. Waugh marveled at this vibrant young culture's potential to replace European Catholicism as the champion in the flowering of a new Christendom. He noted American Catholicism's youthful spirit, its religious fervor, its educational institutions that were accessible to all (contrasted with the English schools of Anglican privilege). He commented on the signs that this minority religion was bursting into bloom: the long

Communion lines, the colorful diversity of immigrant styles and customs, the convents and monasteries full of dedicated men and women.

Tellingly, the most vivid and intensely personal parts of the article have to do with simple rites and devotions he saw carried out, as in an Ash Wednesday service in New Orleans, where "the old grim message" of dust-to-dust was repeated over the signing of the ashes on foreheads, and in the devout practices of African Americans, burdened with harshness and injustice, whom he saw lighting vigil candles and kneeling in humble prayer. For these faithful people, he writes, "the Church has not always been a kind mother."

Waugh also refers to specific Catholics who impressed him, Thomas Merton among them. Merton, he writes, represents the growing cloistered, contemplative movement in the States, then adds: "The Church and the world need monks and nuns more than they need writers. These merely decorate. The Church can get along very well without them."[55] These are exaggerated comments, which Waugh the prolific Catholic writer surely did not believe himself, and they can also be read as a barb directly aimed at Merton, the most famous monk-author in America, who was by now churning out books as fast as his publishers could print them.

Because in letters to friends Waugh made comments that varied to suit the sensibilities of particular correspondents, it is difficult to know exactly what he himself thought of the article. To Nancy Mitford he wrote, "It is a tremendously boring article. . . . That is what they like you see."[56] For Waugh, it was the fulfillment of an obligation, one that did not warrant further musing or commentary on his part.

Dear Mr. Waugh,

OCTOBER 15, 1949
FEAST OF ST TERESA

You will be amused to hear that your article on the "American Epoch in the Catholic Church" is now being read in our refectory, to the accompaniment of some obstreperous coughing by the fathers who have surnames like Flanagan.[57] I like it very much indeed and I think you have handled the situation very well, but fortunately I had already read the article for myself. The treatment to which it is being subjected by this week's reader is atrocious. He announced, for instance, in the introductory note, that you were the author of a best-seller called *Bridgehead Revised*. Really! If they let him get so far as the voting stage (he is a novice) I assure you he gets black from me[58]—unless he wants to change to the lay brothers. The article is well liked by everyone, even by many of the Irish. I imagine your fanmail from the latter is, however, rather hot.[59] I remember a letter I got from a man in Peekskill, New York, for just one innocent little hint that perhaps the Irish sometimes got drunk (which you deleted from the English edition). The man said that he was positively going to send the ancient Order of Hibernians on my trail, declared that my book had "dragged many fine men into the mire," and closed with the woeful words: "Hoping to carry this matter further." I do not know where he carried it, but no repercussions have so far reached the abbey.

I meant to say in my other letter that I appreciated your remarks about the Carthusians. The truth is, I am firmly settled here. Since God has chosen the cenobitic life for me, it is evidently what I most need and then, too, there is really an extraordinary flexibility in our life as it is being led here at the moment. Everyone is ready to accept new suggestions and ideas and we are broadening out in many ways. Did I tell you that Father Abbot now allows me to run off to the woods by myself now? It is a great help. And rather unusual, I think. Then, with the growing numbers, we have been allowed to spread out more within the enclosure itself. We used to be all cooped up in that little garden you saw. Now we can rove around the orchards during the time of spiritual reading, if we want to. So I am quite ready to believe your friend who says that the Cistercians can actually lead a more contemplative life than the Carthusians. We are certainly not hidebound and we are not overburdened with vocal prayers. And that is a burden which is heavier when the prayers are recited in private, I think.

With best wishes and prayers,*
Sincerely yours in Christ,
Fr. M. Louis Merton o.c.r.
*Of course I keep you in my Mass.

6
Waters of Silence

In spite of the serene tone of his October letter to Waugh, by the fall of 1949 Merton was facing important decisions regarding his writing output. The royalties from his books were helping to finance not only the construction of Gethsemani's new additional wings but also the new American Trappist foundations, which in six years had doubled in number (from three to six). The abbot was in no rush to put a stop to the number of Merton books making their way into bookstores. Merton himself was on a roll, exhausting himself as more and more ideas and plans worked their way into book contracts. But he was well aware that the writing quality suffered. Already he was wringing his hands in apology over two of the manuscripts he had written under obedience to Abbot Frederick in his first years of monastic life. They were the biographies of two nuns, written in the pious and hagiographic style of early devotional writers.

As early as the summer of 1948 he had written to his agent Naomi Burton concerning the book about the Trappistine Mother Berchmans, "I am grieved at having

written a book so corney as *Exile Ends in Glory* . . . some
parts of it make me writhe. I apologise. Don't disown me,
please."[60] And informing her of the other one, the story
of the medieval stigmatic St. Lutgarde, and written with
the same pious verbiage, he confessed, "The title is to be
What Are These Wounds, which is what I will be saying
to myself after the critics get hold of it."[61] The cover,
which featured a picture of a nun gazing up in ecstasy
at the pierced foot of Jesus, was destined, Merton said,
to win the critics' golden raspberry award. Together,
Merton and Burton tried to insist that the author's
name on both books should be "Father Louis," so that
the authorship would not be so closely identified with
that of *The Seven Storey Mountain*, but the books had
been contracted to Bruce & Co., a prominent Catholic
publisher, who would not back down. Indeed, the name
"Thomas Merton" was going to be the books' main
selling feature. (A typical sentence in *What Are These
Wounds?* to make Merton writhe with embarrassment
and Waugh throw up his hands: "Whether, as in the case
of the man whom she saved from despair by the mere
light of her countenance, Lutgarde acted by her presence
alone, or whether she gave the benefit of her heavenly
wisdom and her prayers, as she did for example to the
poor to whom she had nothing else to give personally,
or to the young Benedictine priest of Afflighem who was

sent to take charge of a dissolute and intractable parish, St. Lutgarde shed everywhere around her the light of grace and the consolations of the Holy Spirit."[62])

When Waugh wrote in August that hostile critics might no longer take Merton's work seriously, he was stating a concern shared by others in the monk's publishing life. In her New York office, Naomi Burton was alarmed at what she considered a diminishing of the literary merit of his writing. In September she wrote, "For my part I am not only worried about your literary standing but about the amount of good you can do, from the point of view of your religion. . . . If there is an indication of your getting onto a literary conveyer belt, I think the critics will not fail to censure you and you are likely too to reach a saturation point of readers much too quickly."

Not only was Merton suggesting several new books, but he was also proposing that New Directions take on one of the novels that had failed to find a publisher in his premonastic years. She reminded him that the novel had been rejected by six publishers. "You know that I have always admired your writing," she wrote, "but let's face it, the books did not make the grade then, why should they now? Now you are famous, is the answer, of course. I don't like the sound of that answer a little bit."[63] Two months later she sent an even more dire warning: "I think it's quite perilously near the time when you are going to lose readers through over publication."[64] From London, the Hollis and Carter editor Tom Burns wrote to Burton, "A really good book every two or three years would be so much more beneficial in every conceivable way (including financial) than a whole series of lesser products or resuscitated earlier MMS. I know Evelyn Waugh will back me up in this."[65]

Waugh himself wrote to Sister Thérèse Lentfoehr, asking her not to praise Merton too much. "One would like to think of him wrapped in silence, not typing out articles every day," he wrote. "I must admit that I think the writing of *The Waters of Siloe* rather inferior to his earlier work. I don't think it possible to combine a Trappist's life with that of a professional writer. Cheese and liqueurs are the proper products of the contemplative life."[66]

Merton was caught three ways, between his own ideas for books, his superiors' suggestions, and the caution expressed by those who knew the ways of the publishing world. Overworked, beset by the noise of power mowers and other machines outside, perpetually tired, and with little outlet for the solitude he craved, he agreed to slow down the production of books. A reprieve of sorts was thrust upon him: teaching. Abbot James wanted to improve the education of the young monks, and Merton heartily agreed, suggesting a program of studies that would include courses in Scripture, mystical theology, Cistercian studies, and, for future superiors, canon law. In November Merton began giving regular lectures.

Dear Mr. Waugh, JANUARY 28, 1950

It is some time since I have given an account of myself. Burns sent a copy of Fowler and I am very grateful. I am studying it with much amusement and profit. I remember enjoying it when I dipped into it in past years. In those days I was mostly interested in his wit. That Graves and Hodge book is very helpful.

And now comes a matter that belongs to St. Benedict's fifth degree of humility. In spite of the earnest efforts of my abbot, my agent and myself, Bruce and company is bringing forth an atrocious biography of a Cistercian stigmatic that I wrote five years ago under obedience. We did what we could to stop it but it was too late. The thing was sent to them some years ago and the contract was signed too long ago for my own good. I hope a copy of it never falls into your hands. In spite of your great forbearance, you would never forgive me. Please pray that it may not do any harm.

Did I tell you that I am now busy teaching? Perhaps not. It takes up most of my time, but it will serve to accumulate material for biographies and doctrinal studies of St. Bernard and of St. Aelred of Rievaulx. You will be pleased at the thought that I am now working slowly and thoughtfully. I like it above all because it helps me to be a monk instead of a journalist. What I am teaching is Mystical Theology. This year I am on the Cistercians. Next year we hope to have a course in Mystical Theology from Origen to St. John of the Cross. A most wonderful amount of production is being done in France, on the Fathers. Did you see that article in *The Month* on the "Return to Contemplation"?

I have long hesitated to send you a copy of the *Years of the Blind Lions* since you do not like modern poetry, but a copy is on the way as a token of my gratitude for your great kindness in going over *Waters of Siloe.* I am eager to see what the book will be like and know it will be easier reading after your editing. I think, incidentally, that teaching will help me to get direct hits instead of spraying the whole neighborhood of my target, especially when I am trying to talk about doctrine.

In any case, please believe me to be most grateful as always, for your kindness. I remember you often at Mass, asking Our Lord to bless you and your family and your work and all that you do, that you may give Him glory and help to extend His Kingdom on earth. It is a very sobering thing to go each day to the altar to offer this tremendous Sacrifice and one of the principal effects it has had on me has been to leave me convinced that once one has pronounced the words of the Canon there is practically nothing left worth saying—except to wait until next morning's Mass. Do not think, however, that I despise the Postcommunions—or that I walk into class and stare at the young monks in silence and then walk out again in disgust.

As ever,

In Christo Domino,

Fr. M. Louis Merton O.C.R.

Waugh had agreed to repeat his editing job on Merton by preparing *The Waters of Siloe* for British publication, and had spent part of the fall of 1949 in despair over the task. His gracious appreciation of the book had been sincere, but when it came to scrutinizing the text, the flaws stood out dauntingly. He wrote to his Catholic friend Katharine Asquith of his distress over the literary result when a monk, instead of heading out to work in the fields, is "set down at a typewriter and told to produce books."[67] In writing *The Waters of Siloe*, Merton "did not seem to know what he was doing or what he had already done." What should he do as editor, Waugh asked—cut out everything that did not pertain to a history of American Cistercians? Leave the structure as it was, with only the awkward parts edited out? Or—"Publish and be damned?" He concluded: "I find I have bitten off more than my failing teeth can chew."

Although he had expressed these possibilities out of exasperation, he did some of all three. He rearranged two chapters so that the history of the monks, from twelfth-century France to twentieth-century America, flowed chronologically. He excised the whole prologue, the apparently true story of a French businessman who had a miraculous vision of St. Thérèse of Lisieux and later became a Trappist monk—a startling beginning for a straightforward history of the order in the United States and an odd piece of devotional journalism out of step with Merton's usual work. (Twenty years later Merton was still to remember Waugh's ruthless dismissal of it.) He also removed the eight-page "Note on the Function of a Contemplative Order," an apologia that, as Waugh had explained to Merton, he said in a better way elsewhere in the book. Waugh placed in an appendix the monks' timetable, "The Daily Life of a Cistercian Monk in Our Time," which was of general interest rather than part of the history. These structural changes were probably the easiest part of the editing job. As he worked through the text, he edited out vague phrases ("with a show of interest"), casual and unnecessary sentences ("And even there he is recalled less as a saint than as a kind of phenomenon"), words conveying too much emotion and lacking in substance ("marvelous," "tremendous"), as well as the kind of lead-in phrases ("In other words") that Waugh had removed from the earlier book.

By the time Waugh reached chapter eight and the nineteenth-century foundation of Gethsemani, discouragement and boredom overtook him. The rest of the book, nearly half the total number of pages, received little editing. Even overused exclamation marks, which Waugh struck out earlier and which stylists such as Fowler sternly regard as signs of an amateur writer, were allowed to remain. Merton's dedication page, TO EVELYN WAUGH, disappeared. As he had done with *Elected Silence*, Waugh wrote the foreword to the British publication of the new book. It covers little more than half a page: nineteen lines, all in one paragraph. Depending on how one reads it, the foreword is either a gracious attempt on Waugh's part to do a gallant service on behalf of the monk-author (a gesture of which he was often capable), or a backhanded compliment. In writing it, Waugh seemed to be facing his own criticism of the book and of Merton's writing life itself—criticisms he had articulated in letters to Sister Thérèse Lentfoehr and Katharine Asquith. "Many critics have expressed surprise that a Trappist monk should write—and publish his writings," Waugh writes in the foreword, as if trying to preempt such criticism. Although this was the opinion Waugh had begun to espouse, he declared it "a romantic and untheological view of the character of the contemplative life." Monks must earn their living, usually by manual work (as he had written to Mrs. Asquith), but, he argued, Merton's "energies are best employed at the typewriter." He added laconically (and perhaps drily), "We may therefore expect a number of books from him in the future."

The point Waugh had made to Sister Thérèse, that monks should stick to making cheese and liqueur, he now argued against: "Now we have the opportunity of reading works designed to popularise the idea of the contemplative life. It is not for us, living in the world, to cavil at this generous decision." The last two sentences cut to the heart of Waugh's critique of Merton's machinelike writing process, where readership was not thought through, and where the words were tapped onto a page without benefit of second thoughts or critical assessment.

One can ask the question too: Did Merton's writing, especially that of *Seeds of Contemplation*, strike too close to Waugh's spiritual center, opening up an area of discomfort that was too much for Waugh to examine? His final sentence in the foreword, and his final public statement on the work of Thomas Merton—"It is not for us, living in the world, to cavil at this generous decision."—juxtaposes "cavil," which suggests pettiness and crankiness, with "generous," which points to openness and large-heartedness. Is there a struggle within him as he faces the monk on the other side of the Atlantic Ocean who, against everyone's advice, is going to keep on writing and searching his own depths?

Regardless of Waugh's own inner disposition, however, he knew that his assertion about Merton, "We may . . . expect a number of books from him in the future," was one he could safely make without being proved wrong.

The British title of the book was changed from *The Waters of Siloe* to *The Waters of Silence*. The new title, like *Elected Silence*, reflects Waugh's preference for clarity. Taken together with *Elected Silence*, the title also echoes Waugh's preferred status for Merton—"wrapped in silence." This provides one more indication of what Waugh considered essential to the monastic life and, perhaps, his disillusionment with the most famous of its proponents. Despite his opinion of Merton's writing and the decision to combine the vocation of a monk with that of a writer, Waugh's final few letters to Merton continue to reflect a warm friendliness.

7

"I keep you occasionally in my Mass"

AUGUST 1950 – FEBRUARY 1952

Waugh returned to his fiction writing in 1949, and his first novel since *Brideshead Revisited* was published in 1950. It was called *Helena*, an imagined account (or a legend, as he described it himself) of the life of St. Helen, the mother of the emperor Constantine. Even as he was writing it, *Helena* became his favorite of all his works of fiction. The short novel was excerpted over June and July of 1950 in issues of the British Jesuit journal *The Month*.

The Waters of Silence, too, was published in the summer of 1950. A review in *The Spectator* noted Merton's somber conclusion as he surveyed the centuries of his order: that few within it seeking the contemplative life had been able to attain it because of political and religious hostilities in the first instance and material business in the second. The reviewer also zeroed in on an observation similar to one of Waugh's complaints: that Merton's style "is compounded of dignity and impudence." He quoted two examples of the latter: "The contemplative spirit caved in" and, with reference to a contemporary monk, the man was to be seen "sinking his teeth . . . into his Cistercian vocation."[68] There is no hint that the reviewer knew of Evelyn Waugh's editorship of the book, and it is likely that Waugh kept quiet about his involvement in any part of *The Waters of Silence*, apart from writing the foreword.

Dear Mr. Waugh:

Hollis and Carter have just sent me *Waters of Silence,* with your kind foreword and your expert editing. It was a much more difficult piece of work for you to reshape than *Elected Silence,* but I am deeply indebted to you for doing such a good job. I have no regrets at the cutting of the Prologue and am glad it went. The opening story never sat very comfortably on my conscience. The defence of my ideas about the contemplative life was quite useless and I have done it properly, in any case, in an article for *Cross and Crown.*[69] That was where the defence belonged.

Thank you especially for your foreword. I do not know whether the amount of books against which you warn the reader, will ever be produced. I am working slowly at them and I am also teaching now. The teaching serves to accumulate material for books but does not allow me as much time for writing as I need. Your remark about life in the Scriptorium being harder is, as a matter of fact, no fancy, as I am beginning to discover after seven years of it. (My first year in the monastery was the only one when I went out every day). However, I do get out into the fields occasionally. For the first time in eight years I have been able to do something that might reasonably be called "bathing," when I managed to fell a tree in such a way that it dropped across a stream. That made it necessary to get in the water to trim it and cut it up. Very pleasant. I shall try to get out again before they finish cutting down all the trees along that creek.

Helena looks fine, in The Month. I especially admire your dialogue—the most difficult thing in a historical novel, isn't it? But above all I was delighted by the witch's little song.

It has occurred to me several times that in one of my other letters I may have said something that offended you. I do hope this is not so, but if it is, I know you will forgive me. Perhaps you have had wind of that hideous book I did, on a mediaeval stigmatic. I can understand your being vexed at the appearance of such a thing (the publisher gave it an abominable presentation too), when you had come out on a limb to assure people that I deserved some respect. We tried to keep the thing from being printed but the idea occurred to us too late.

I think it is being printed in Ireland. I hope that you will not be splashed by the mud that may be thrown at it. But really I don't think it will reach the kind of people who really care about the difference between a good book and a bad one.

Soon I hope to be able to send you a new, short book that is coming out, called *Bread in the Wilderness*. It is about the Psalms, and I hope you will like it. It is a little technical but I hope it is not dry.

I frequently remember you at Mass, and pray Our Lord to repay you for all your kindness. It is not to me that you have been kind but to Him especially. And if my books have reached people in England and have done them any good, most of the credit goes to you. May Our Lady ever be with you and help you to do much for the glory of her Son.

Sincerely in Corde Christi,
Fr. M. Louis Merton

PS. Looking back at one of your letters I found you said you were send-ing a volume of sermons by Mgr. Knox—I have no knowledge of their ever having arrived. About the Gardeil book[70] which you were trying to get for us: since it is so unobtainable we finally got it on microfilm. That was our only hope. But thanks very much for your efforts.

Most of Waugh's letters to Merton were written on plain writing paper with a logo consisting of his home address, which at the time was Piers Court in Gloucestershire. His next letter was written on paper with a thick gold Italianate border. The centerpiece at the top was a figure of the child Jesus dressed in colored robes with his heart exposed. Beneath this picture, attached by an accordion-type pleat so that it bobbed up and down, was one of the infant Jesus in a manger. The two paintings were of the bad-taste devotional sort that both writers despised. Waugh had spent several weeks during the spring in Italy, traveling alone. (His wife was pregnant with their seventh child.) His purported reason was Pope Pius XII's proclamation of 1950 as a "Holy Year." He spent Easter in Rome and visited friends, among other activities, trying (without success) through various papal connections to get permission for a private chapel at Piers Court. He told Merton that the extravagant notepaper came from Naples.

Enclosed with his letter was a clipping of a review from *The Times Literary Supplement. The Waters of Silence*, the review claimed, did not stand up to the spiritual classics of authors such as John Henry Newman and St. Teresa, but the book was "a pleasant, sincere, and readable book, which leaves behind it an impression of strenuous piety rather than of mystical vision."[71] It was the sort of faint-praise assessment to make a writer cringe, although Merton did not comment on it. The unnamed author of the article went on to ask, as Waugh and others had before him, why a Trappist was writing a book at all if that particular form of monastic life was intended to be hidden in prayer. The article concluded, "if the waters of silence are to run deep, logic would have it that the silence must be of the pen as well as of the tongue."

Dear Fr. Louis, AUGUST 30, 1950

Of course you have never said anything that remotely "offended" me. How could you think so? I can only suppose that my general bad temper crept into my correspondence. Please forgive me.

It is extraordinarily generous of you to take my editing of *Waters of Siloe* in such good part. (I was paid in church candles for the dining room table.) It was a difficult book to prepare for the European reader who doesn't like discursive writing nowadays. . . .

I am delighted that you liked *Helena*. I will send you a copy in October. I hope it has a safer voyage than the Knox sermons. . . . I am particularly glad you approved of the witches' song. . . .

I have had another son born since last writing to you—named Septimus. (We have one child who died in infancy).

I expect to be in New York for a brief visit in October. Too brief, I am afraid, to hope to get to Kentucky.

Yours ever,
Evelyn Waugh

By the fall of 1950, the crowding of monks brought about by the influx of candidates for the novitiate meant that new wings and new buildings had to be built. The noise of construction that followed added to Merton's frustration and exhaustion. His new responsibilities as a teacher of theology, in addition to the residual work on several publishing projects, had begun to take its toll. During the winter, there had been one epidemic of influenza after another in the monastery, and Merton was not spared. Insomnia was a constant problem, and he had begun having trouble breathing. The stomach complaints that had plagued him for months grew worse. The decision was made for him to undergo tests at St. Joseph's Infirmary in Louisville.

Dear Mr. Waugh: SEPT. 11TH 1950

The Stromboli note-paper literally overwhelmed me. I am answering you at once to send my congratulations on the advent of Septimus and to assure you that the entire choir-novitiate here is praying for him with enthusiasm. So too am I.

Then, I enclose a monument of American Catholic endeavor.[72] A copy of this leaflet was addressed to every priest in the community here, but was, of course, stopped by the censor. I managed to get one for your archives. It is really something, isn't it?

I am just off to the hospital, but am not especially ill. The doctors seem to think their time has come to compass me with devices. They believe that they can produce ulcers by this method: ulcers being what they intend to find. If they succeed I shall sink back in mournful resignation at the thought that I have reached a rather un-monastic middle age.[73]

In our Orientation course for the novices I have been working on the Desert Fathers and think they would be a wonderful subject for a book. Have you ever thought of trying it? You know the country, of course. But if you do not do it, I hope that some day I will get a chance to try. But you could do a wonderful job on them.

I must now close and tidy up, before they carry me off.

Yours in Corde Christi,
Fr. M. Louis O.C.R.

Thank you very much for the review—the first and only one I had seen. I am presuming you do not want it back as it might make this letter too heavy.

~⁓

Waugh returned to the United States in October of 1950 for an eighteen-day visit. The trip was primarily intended as a vacation for Laura after the birth of their seventh child, but it proved to be a change as well for Waugh, who had become depressed as he approached the age of fifty. *Helena* had garnered only moderate sales, and he was disappointed with the lukewarm reviews of the novel, which he would continue to regard as his best book. They spent their time visiting friends in New York. Waugh was in his element. An expat friend, Anne Fremantle, wrote to him on his return to England, "You touch these shores, & presto, life is a party & we all dance as though at the Waterloo Eve Ball."[74]

Merton spent the fall months in and out of St. Joseph's Infirmary in Louisville. His hospitalization sessions culminated in surgery on his nose to relieve his breathing, but colitis continued to afflict him. The enforced rest, however, left him feeling restored.

Dear Mr. Waugh,

This letter has two purposes: to thank you for *Helena* and to wish you a holy Christmas—and even a merry one, although the legend is abroad that I have gone Jansenist.

Helena came when I was in the hospital. It was handed to me on the afternoon of the day when I had had three inches of bone cut out of my nose and was parked in bed with a nose full of bandages, commanded to sit up for twenty four hours behaving in all respects like Queen Victoria. It was then that I started in on Old King Coel.[75] I compliment you on your fidelity to the traditional picture of this King. Unfortunately, your use of the famous ballad almost made me have a haemmhorage [sic] (if that is how you spell it.) I am afraid that those on this side of the Atlantic who have never sung it will miss some of the nicest pages in the book.

I mentioned a legend about myself. There is another one that is more colorful. A certain Robert Louis, who tossed an atomic bomb on Hiroshima, I believe, entered a monastery somewhere. One day, a visitor to a slightly deaf nun in a convent hereabouts remarked: "Robert Louis has entered a monastery. He's the one who threw the atomic bomb and killed sixty thousand people." The nun let out a faint scream and rushed into the convent returning presently with the whole community . . . "Father Louis . . . who is in the Trappist monastery . . . threw an atomic bomb . . . etc. etc." Nice reputation I have.

I beg God to bless you and all your family *a primo usque ad Septimum* ["from the oldest down to Septimus"]. May you enjoy all the graces of Christmas. It is my intention to remember you all in my Christmas Masses. Pray for me too, please.

Yours ever in Christ,
Fr. M. Louis o.c.s.o.

Waugh had become concerned about the status of the Christian holy places in the postwar Arab Middle East and the new state of Israel, and he persuaded *Life* to finance a trip to the Holy Land. He set out in January of 1951 for Israel, Jordan, Syria, and Turkey, the highlight of which was an all-night vigil inside the Church of the Holy Sepulchre. There, he was moved by being at the historic epicenter of Christendom, by the mingling of devout pilgrims and the priests in fearsome garb chanting their ancient rites. The result of the trip was an article called "Defence of the Holy Places," which was published in *Life* in the issue of December 24, 1951, and later became a book.

Waugh wrote the following on a note card. It was obviously written in haste, with no salutation and no date.

[PROBABLY JANUARY 1951]

. . . Does your library possess or have you read Ronnie Knox's new mouthpiece, . . . *Enthusiasm.*[76] It is a book made especially for you. . . . Let me know quickly as I am just off to Holy Land.

E.W.

Merton's ninth book, *The Ascent to Truth*, was published in 1951. (*Bread in the Wilderness*, which he had promised to Waugh, did not appear until 1953.) His most ambitious spiritual work yet, *The Ascent* was an examination of the mystical doctrine of St. John of the Cross. He had begun writing it three years earlier, describing it at first as a theology of contemplation. Its development had been a torturous effort for him. The manuscript had gone through at least two different titles as it progressed and, from time to time, gave Merton an anxious (and highly unusual) case of writer's block.

In the spring of 1951 a scholasticate was created at Gethsemani: a period of time similar to that in other male religious orders when the young men who have made vows prepare for the priesthood. It was another step forward at the abbey in acknowledging the large numbers of newly professed monks and their need for further education and spiritual formation. Merton was named the new Master of Scholastics. For the time being, he now described himself as the spiritual director of twenty-five young men, and no longer a writer.

Waugh, in the meantime, began reading the diaries he had kept while serving with the British armed forces during the war, and from them began the first pages toward what would become the first volume of his war trilogy, *Men at Arms*. He also continued giving copious writing advice to those who asked for it. Merton had not asked for it, but Waugh, with his keen sense of prose structure and readership, still considered the monk as a student of writing, and he ventured forth anyway. His letters to Merton were always written in a courteous tone, and this, his last, is no exception. He begins by saying not only how touched he is by the gift of *The Ascent to Truth*, but also that he values it more than any other present he has received that year. And then, in a sense, he rolls up his sleeves.

Dear Fr. Louis,   DECEMBER 27, 1951

. . . *The Ascent* is a most impressive work. I hope it is having the success it deserves.

May I venture one criticism? I will not of course do anything but applaud the subject . . . but since you patiently listened to some technical advice in the past, may I say this?

I think it is a fault with the work in some of your later writing, that you do not seem to have decided whom precisely you are addressing. You must, I am sure, in the writing have a specific reader in mind. In *The Ascent* are you writing (a) for the "good Catholic" who has never attempted the higher forms of prayer and knows St. John of the Cross only by name, or (b) the literary man who has read St. John as part of the general equipment of philosophic education but now misunderstands him through not having the Faith, (c) the religious who have attempted higher forms of prayer but have failed, (d) specialists on mystical writing, in order to draw their attention to aspects of St. John which strike you as neglected or misinter-preted?

. . . You seem to wander from page to page between the four of them, now taking the ignorant (like myself) right out of his depth, now offering rudimentary information which is quite superfluous to other categories.

For example, you use "aphotic"[77] with the casual hint that it means "dark." . . . If you use words like that without a footnote you are obviously addressing specialists. Yet the next chapter might be a talk to a youth club.

So, too, with "We." You use it constantly but seldom in the same sense—sometimes as meaning priests in their teaching capacity, sometimes the whole world.

I do think the power of your writing would be greatly increased if you decided on a single level for each book—or write four books instead of one explaining the same matter to the four categories I have suggested. . . .

I am just coming to the end of the first volume of what I hope will be a series of works covering the whole of the last war.[78] It has some good bits of pure farce but much that is dull and trite.

Ever yours very sincerely
Evelyn Waugh

It is puzzling that Merton kept on sending his books to Waugh, knowing that he would receive criticism in equal measure to gratitude. He did not expressly request critiques from the novelist, and so this gesture may have been one way of keeping the friendship alive and at the same time offering spiritual help to Waugh. By now, however, life at Gethsemani had undergone subtle changes. In addition to giving lectures to the novices and taking charge of the monks who were studying for the priesthood, he had been given permission to roam the woods and fields in search of solitude. Yet his restless mind refused to stay put. This may be one reason why his correspondence with Evelyn Waugh was soon to come to an end.

Dear Mr. Waugh,   FEBRUARY 25, 1952

Many thanks for your very kind letter and for *Enthusiasm*. I entirely agree with your comment on the patchy character of *The Ascent*. It is getting to be increasingly difficult to get a book together at all, and I know very well that the chapter on "The Problem of Unbelief" was addressed to a different "reader" than the others, while two other early chapters were originally intended for a completely different book!! I tried to drop the "Problem" chapter but the publisher wanted to keep it as bait for this apologetically minded nation. I suppose it is the one chapter that has more or less registered—at least with the clergy.

When I say that it is hard to put a book together I do not mean that I have gone to seed (although maybe as a writer I have—and perhaps it is a good thing). But I have so many other things to do now that I cannot write anything except fragmentary sentences. I am Director of the scholastics. This is very fine. I talk to them about their problems. With some of them I have an agreement that I occasionally write out cryptic ascetic sentences in the Desert Father tradition and slip the paper to them when they least expect it. Then they go away and think about these statements of mine. They could make a book. But

I don't know if it would be a stuffy book or not. There again, you have a scattered audience.

Enthusiasm is fine. I value it highly above all as a reference book, but it is also very good reading. I promise myself to make it an arsenal if I return to writing about quietists.[79] The Procurator General of the Carthusians says I am too sharp on quietists and that there really are no quietists anyway. But it is to me a guarantee that the Jesuits will not be too angry with anything I say about contemplation if I drub the quietists for a few pages in every book. Besides, I have the same baleful interest in quietism that a doctor might have in chiropractors or a MFH[80] in people who shoot foxes.

Your article on the Holy Land was read in the refectory and I thought it was the best piece of reporting you have done. I especially enjoyed the description of the Holy Sepulchre at night. Did you get any closer to the Abyssinians[81] on the roof? Did you see the Greek monastery on the "Mountain of the Temptation"—is it still there? Did you run into anything connected with this Charbel Makhlouf[82] in Syria? I have a piece of wood from Charles de Foucauld's[83] hermitage in Nazareth and I am getting ready to plant it secretly in the forest here, in the hope that a small hermitage will spring up after the rains in April.

Actually, what I *am* going to do, beginning next week, is to go out to the forest with a crew of novices every day, planting some twelve thousand pine seedlings where we have been cutting a lot of timber. That, I think, is going to be very pleasant.

About *apophatic*—although it is not in the OED[84] it does crop up in English, though in translations of French books like Mgr. Journet's "Dark Knowledge of God." That word has however caused more trouble than almost anything else in the *Ascent*.

God bless you always and all your family. I keep you occasionally in my Mass.

Sincerely in Christ,
Fr . M Louis

"A crusty old man"

Merton's letter of February 25, 1952, is the last of the extant correspondence between him and Waugh. Why did the friendship of these two illustrious Catholic writers peter out? Merton still showed signs of the student eager to learn from the master, but he had also begun to grow up as a writer and was prepared to express disagreement with Waugh on certain matters of style. He had developed confidence in his own natural gift as a writer. Besides, he was receiving bags of letters from grateful readers telling him how helpful his books were to them. He was not writing in a stilted manner of an earlier era, as if the spiritual life sat apart from the rest of life in the mid-twentieth century, but in a casual and colloquial language, often laced with humor. Whatever his books lacked in literary excellence, they made up for in insight and freshness of approach.

Merton's desire for greater solitude and his leaning toward a move to the Carthusians or the Camaldolese, another contemplative religious order, continued throughout the 1950s. In 1965 he received long-sought permission to live permanently in a hermitage, a plain cottage built of cinder blocks, on monastery grounds but some distance away from the main buildings. His interests, however, had expanded beyond Gethsemani. The monastery no longer was the haven, the only place where he could find God. In 1948, after a doctor's visit to Louisville, he wrote in his journal that he was disgusted with that city. A decade later, he had a revelatory moment while standing on an ordinary street corner, Fourth and Walnut, in downtown Louisville: a realization that he belonged together with all the people around him who were going on about their own business, not realizing that they were all together among the righteous in Jesus's parable of the sower of the seed and were "shining like the sun" (Matt. 13:43).

He himself later described most of the 1950s as years of transition, and he named *Disputed Questions*, a book of essays on the history of the spiritual life, first published in 1953, as the beginning of a new phase in his writing life. In the preface to that book, he warns the reader that it is neither an "inspirational" book nor a philosophical treatise, but a study of particular spiritual questions that have been preoccupying him for some time. But the questions are not meant merely for the individual spiritual life; they also touch on social issues of the day—specifically the Cold War and totalitarian governments. By the early 1960s the monastery itself had softened its ascetical, penitential rules somewhat in favor of the more contemplative way of life (much of the move due to Merton's influence).

In later years, Merton distanced himself from the author of *The Seven Storey Mountain*, the book that had so impressed Evelyn Waugh. His early monastic experiences, he said, were those of a first conversion, and thus his attitude to the Christian vocation at the time was one of "us and them," with a strict separation between the things of God and the things of the world. As the years went on he continued to ponder ambivalently on his life as a writer. In an undated essay, probably written in the mid-1950s, even as several Merton titles were rolling off the press, he wrote, "I think the writer ought to dedicate his life to God, live in a cave, write all the year round and then tear up all he has written at the end of the year, the way the Desert Fathers used to weave baskets as they prayed and then take them all apart. For it is not the weaving that matters, but the praying, and writing after all can be a form of prayer."[85]

He had begun reading psychology and secular philosophy, the works of other Christians and of practitioners of eastern traditions, especially Zen Buddhism. Then with the 1960s, he became aware of the nuclear bomb and the question of racial inequality in America. The number of his correspondents increased, and his circle of friends became wider. Naomi Burton's prediction that he was becoming overexposed as a writer was proved wrong, over and over again, but her worry—and Waugh's—about the unevenness in the literary quality of his work has found echoes in other critics over the decades. (The prior of the Benedictine Portsmouth Abbey, Aelred Graham, was an early critic, writing in the pages of the *Atlantic Monthly*: "A practiced writer, [Merton] achieves in prose the merits of force and clarity; but it is too highly charged, too diffuse and uneven, to attain distinction."[86]) As in Merton's early years, with the proliferation of articles and books, there was always a tug-of-war between his creative growth—always moving, always changing—and his desire for greater solitude and silence.

By the 1950s Waugh's passionate interest in American Catholic monasticism had disappeared. His short visit to the United States in the fall of 1950 was his last. Just under two years after he had told a reporter that Gethsemani Abbey had impressed him more than anything else in America, he traveled no farther than New York City on this trip. He completed the third volume of his war trilogy (the three together called *Sword of Honour*) in 1961. It was his last novel and has been considered by many to be the best work of fiction coming out of the Second World War. His hero of the trilogy, Guy Crouchback, is a hapless officer, wronged by his wife and by the military life he finds himself in, and emerges as a model of Christian fortitude and charity: the kind of Christian that Waugh himself would have liked to be.

For Waugh, melancholy began to set in as health problems beset him, and he became physically enfeebled. On January 3, 1954, a Sunday, he wrote in his diary, "Church again. My prayer is now only, 'Here I am again. Show me what to do; help me do it.'"[87] However cold and dry, it was a prayer that Merton—and most of the saints—would have recognized as their own at one time or another.

With the 1960s, the world and the Catholic Church seemed to leave Evelyn Waugh behind. His final years were filled with bitterness over the changes the church was making: the rock he had relied on for his own stability seemed no longer solid. He took as much solace as he could from the Latin Mass and the Jesuit and Benedictine friends he had always relied on. The Second Vatican Council, a breath of badly needed fresh air to most Catholics, rang the death knell of the Catholicism Waugh knew and loved. Even before the council there were signs of change: in the mid-fifties the centuries-old Holy Week services, culminating in the Easter Triduum that he observed as a mainstay of the faith every year at Downside Abbey, were altered so as to be closer to the practice of the early church. The new dispensation was as gall to him.

Still, Waugh knew his Christian priorities. When in a 1960 BBC interview he was asked how he would like to be remembered after his death, his reply was, "I would like people in their charity to pray for my soul as a sinner."[88] Years earlier, he may have had himself in mind when, in his novel, *Brideshead Revisited*, he had Cordelia, the sister of the alcoholic renegade Sebastian Flyte, say that her brother and others like him "are very near and dear to God." And perhaps he was thinking of himself even further when he had the other sister, Julia, say, "the worse I am, the more I need God. I can't shut myself out from his mercy." Julia's desire for God's mercy was no different from Merton's expressed need throughout his whole monastic life.

By the mid-sixties, Evelyn Waugh was seriously depressed and unwell, his presence casting gloom. Life was no longer a party in his company, and he was no longer the writer of witty, sparkling prose. Thomas Merton, however, remained in his prime, still writing and restlessly looking for a place of solitude. He noted in an August 1964 journal entry that in the magazine *Commonweal* he had read a letter to the editor written by "a crusty old man called Evelyn Waugh." The novelist's letter had reacted to a *Commonweal* article that denounced Catholic conservatism. Merton continued: "I understand conservatism—he is one of the genuine conservatives: he wishes to conserve not what might be lost but what is not even threatened because it vanished long ago."[89]

Had the two been young men together, callow and self-indulgent in their view of the modern world, yet insightful critics and, above all, creative artists hungry for the things of God, they might have become long-lasting friends. They might have discovered the Roman Catholic Church together, recognizing the sanctity and beauty that could be found there, holding onto it as a beacon pointing toward eternity. But the bohemian whom Waugh glimpsed inside the Trappist habit at their one face-to-face meeting would have clashed at some point with the established order that was essential to Waugh's world. Merton was too restless and his mind too active to hold onto any one form for long. Six months before his death he described himself as still evolving, and he had already turned to the East as a source of spiritual riches. Waugh was simply depleted and worn out before his time.

The final straw of the Catholic Church's bow to modernity, for Waugh, was the radical change in the outward form of the Mass. The liturgy he had loved from the time of his conversion was a silent ritual, "the spectacle of the priest and his server . . . stumping up to the altar without a glance to discover how many or how few he had in his congregation; a craftsman and his apprentice; a man with a job which he alone was qualified to do."[90] He wrote this in a despairing exchange of letters with the archbishop of Westminster, Cardinal Heenan, during the last two years of his life. In a later letter he wrote, "Every attendance at Mass leaves me without comfort or edification. I shall never, pray God, apostatize, but church-going is now a bitter trial."[91] His longtime spiritual mentor, the Jesuit Martin D'Arcy, worried that he might abandon the faith.

Waugh's books continued to sell, however, and over the subsequent decades he has been hailed as one of the twentieth century's best writers of English prose. Films have made some of his books even better known over the years. *Elected Silence*, however, his edited version of Merton's *magnum opus*, eventually fell out of print, and if anyone in Britain wants to buy the Trappist's autobiography today, it is *The Seven Storey Mountain*, in its original American published form, that they will find. Merton's best-known books, of course, have never gone out of print.

The two men died, in the end, only two years and eight months apart, each on a significant day. Although Waugh's decline had been long and sad, he died quickly, of coronary thrombosis, in the bathroom of his home. It was Easter Sunday, April 10, 1966. He had just taken part in what for him was the greatest of all consolations: the pre-Vatican II Tridentine Mass, in full Latin.

On Merton's way to the East in the fall of 1968, he looked for a place en route where he might set up a hermitage, and the locations he seemed most interested in were in Alaska and Northern California, as far to the edge of America as he could go. In the ensuing weeks he had broad and deep experiences as he drank from the spiritual waters of the East. His last day of life, however, was spent in his Trappist habit, among similarly garbed Christian monks and nuns, at a conference in Bangkok on Christian monastic renewal. He, too, died quickly, of an electric shock from a defective fan in his room. It was December 10, 1968, the twenty-seventh anniversary of his entrance to Gethsemani.

The manner of each writer's death has formed part of the lore of his life, and significance is to be found in all the details. Their writings, however, disparate as they are, reflect their authors' search for the absolute. These are still, long after their deaths, explored and loved.

1 Thomas Merton, *The Secular Journal of Thomas Merton* (New York: Image, 1959), 198.

2 *My Argument With the Gestapo* was published by New Directions a year after Merton's death. It is generally acknowledged to be more successful as a cryptic glimpse into a part of Merton's early life than as a novel.

3 David D. Cooper, ed., *Thomas Merton and James Laughlin: Selected Letters* (New York: W. W. Norton, 1997), 10.

4 Ibid., 11.

5 William H. Shannon, *Silent Lamp: The Thomas Merton Story* (New York: Crossroad, 1992), 133.

6 Thomas Merton, *The Journals of Thomas Merton*, vol. 2, *Entering the Silence* (San Francisco: HarperSanFrancisco, 1996), 34.

7 Undated, Archives of the British Province of the Society of Jesus.

8 Evelyn Waugh, "Fan-Fare," in *The Essays, Articles and Reviews of Evelyn Waugh*, ed. Donat Gallagher (London: Methuen, 1983), 300.

9 Merton, *Entering the Silence*, 232.

10 Tom Burns was the publisher at Hollis and Carter, and a friend of Waugh's.

11 Evelyn Waugh, *The Diaries of Evelyn Waugh*, ed., Michael Davie (London: Weidenfeld & Nicolson, 1976), 700.

12 This letter, at one time in the archives of the Abbey of Gethsemani, seems to have been lost. Efforts to locate it have been fruitless.

13 The poem "For My Brother: Reported Missing in Action, 1943" concludes part 3 of *The Seven Storey Mountain*.

14 *The Waters of Siloe*.

15 Merton did not know that Evelyn Waugh held *Ulysses,* by James Joyce, in disdain, referring to it as "gibberish" in a television interview in later years. Merton was thus unfortunately unaware of the irony of including Ulysses in the same enthusiastic sentence as Waugh's two great early novels.

16 Although Waugh referred to Merton as "Tom Merton" in his diary entry, he always addressed him personally as "Brother [and later Father] Louis."

17 Christopher Hollis (1902–77) was a convert to Roman Catholicism and a writer friend of Evelyn Waugh's. Waugh served as a mentor to Hollis. He was also a partner in the publishing firm Hollis and Carter.

18 "One stayed up all night, and finally went to sleep wherever there happened to be room for one man to put his tired carcass. . . . I suppose I got some five or six hours of fitful sleep, and at about eleven we were all awake, sitting around disheveled and half stupefied, talking and smoking and playing records" Thomas Merton, *The Seven Storey Mountain* (New York: Harcourt Brace Jovanovich, 1976), 252.

19 Dom Frederic Dunne died on August 4, 1948, and Dom James Fox was elected abbot. He and Merton were to have a complicated relationship, lasting almost until Merton's death.

20 Dom Gabriel Sortais.

21 This manuscript would become *The Waters of Siloe.*

22 Ronald Knox (1888–1957) was a writer and a close friend of Evelyn Waugh. In his reply to Merton's first letter to him, Waugh had indicated that Knox found it hard to believe that God was interested in good prose. Perhaps in deference to his priestly friend's opinion, he considered his own perfectionistic attitude to writing to be a matter of pride.

23 Dom Humphrey Pawsey, O.CART., was a monk of the Carthusian charterhouse at Parkminster, West Sussex, England. He later became the superior of the Charterhouse of the Transfiguration at Sky Farm, Vermont.

24 Mark Amory, ed., *The Letters of Evelyn Waugh* (London: Weidenfeld & Nicolson, 1980), 263.

25 Ibid., 290.

26 Ibid.

27 Merton, *Entering the Silence*, 246.

28 Letter from Merton to Paul A. Doyle, editor of the Evelyn Waugh Newsletter, June 5, 1968, Section A—Correspondence, The Thomas Merton Center at Bellarmine University, Louisville KY.

29 Ibid.

30 Merton, *The Seven Storey Mountain* (hereafter *SSM*), 202; *Elected Silence* (hereafter *ES*), London: Burns & Oates, 1949), 131.

31 *SSM* 163; *ES* 111.

32 *SSM* 14; *ES* 18.

33 *SSM* 231; *ES* 150.

34 *SSM* 15; *ES* 18.

35 *SSM* 176.

36 *SSM* 164; *ES* 112.

37 *ES* 5.

38 *SSM* 161.

39 *ES* 110.

40 Martin Stannard, *Evelyn Waugh: No Abiding City 1939–1966* (London: J. M. Dent, 1992), 270.

41 *Seeds of Contemplation.*

42 "Impressions of a Necrophile," *Washington Post*, February 13, 1949, quoted in Jeffrey Manley and John McGinty, "'Something Entirely Unique': Evelyn Waugh's 1948–49 Tours of North America, Part 2, The Lecture Tour," *Evelyn Waugh Studies* 43, no. 3 (spring 2013).

43 Quoted in Manley and McGinty, "Something Entirely Unique."

44 Ibid.

45 Ibid.

46 Sister Thérèse Lentfoehr, "My Meeting with Evelyn Waugh," *Evelyn Waugh Newsletter* 11 no. 1 (spring, 1977).

47 Quoted in "'Something Entirely Unique': Evelyn Waugh's 1948–49 Tours of North America, Part 2, The Lecture Tour."

48 Thomas Merton, *Seeds of Contemplation* (Norfolk, CT: New Directions, 1949), 140.

49 This was obviously the same religious gadget that Waugh had given out at the Milwaukee lecture.

50 Amory, *Letters of Evelyn Waugh*, April 12, 1949.

51 *The Month*, a journal produced by the British Jesuits, published excerpts of *Elected Silence* in its March and April 1949 editions.

52 This rumor had come to Merton in a letter from a Dominican nun, Sister Marialein. In fact, during the abbot general's visit he had briefly considered taking Merton back to the generalate in Rome. Abbot James Fox strenuously objected.

53 *What Are These Wounds?*

54 Fowler's *Modern English Usage.*

55 Waugh, *Essays, Articles and Reviews*, 387.

56 Amory, *The Letters of Evelyn Waugh*, August 29, 1949, 307.

57 The article made several uncomplimentary statements about Irish Americans.

58 The process of admitting a candidate to the vows involved having each professed monk place a black or a white ball into a vessel as an indication of whether the monk thought the candidate suitable.

59 In the article, Waugh was critical of the cultish attitude among Irish Catholics in America.

60 Unpublished letter, July 9, 1948, Naomi Burton Stone Collection, St. Bonaventure's University Archives, St. Bonaventure, NY.

61 Unpublished letter, January 14, 1950. Ibid.

62 Thomas Merton, *What Are These Wounds?* (Milwaukee: Bruce, 1948), 91.

63 Unpublished letter, September 27, 1949, St. Bonaventure's University Archives, St. Bonaventure, NY.

64 Unpublished letter, November 23, 1949.

65 Unpublished letter, November 15, 1949.

66 Evelyn Waugh, letter to Sister Thérèse Lentfoehr, *Evelyn Waugh Newsletter* 11, no. 1 (spring 1977).

67 Amory, *Letters of Evelyn Waugh*, September 13, 1949, 309.

68 *The Spectator*, November 17, 1950, 28, http://archive.spectator.co.uk/article/17th-november-1950/28/waters-of-silence-by-thomas-merton-hollis-and-cart, accessed 9 December 2014.

69 The article, called "The Primacy of Contemplation," appeared in *Cross and Crown: A Thomistic Quarterly of Spiritual Theology* 2 (1950).

70 Waugh had promised, probably during his visit to Gethsemani, to send Merton a copy of *La Structure de l'âme et l'expérience mystique*. In a letter to Nancy Mitford of January 10, 1949, he asks her to look for it in Paris, where she lived.

71 "The Contemplative Life," *The Times Literary Supplement*, August 11, 1950.

72 Unknown.

73 Merton's medical problem at the time seems to have been a spastic colon.

74 October 29, 1950, quoted in Stannard, *No Abiding City*, 269.

75 According to the legend that Waugh used in *Helena*, Coel was the king of the Trinovantes tribe in ancient Britain.

76 *Enthusiasm* is a history of Christian religious movements. Knox dedicated it to Evelyn Waugh.

77 Waugh obviously misread the word, which was "apophatic."

78 *Men At Arms*, the first volume of the *Sword of Honour* war trilogy.

79 Quietism was a controversial seventeenth-century movement that emphasized God's action in a passive individual soul. The subject of quietism takes up two chapters of *Enthusiasm*.

80 Master of Fox Hounds.

81 Ethiopian monks have the right to live on the roof of the Church of the Holy Sepulchre.

82 Charbel Makhlouf (1828–98) was a monk of the Maronite rite who spent his last years as a hermit. He was canonized in 1977.

83 Charles de Foucauld was a hermit who lived in Nazareth and then in the Sahara Desert, where he was murdered in 1916.

84 Oxford English Dictionary.

85 Thomas Merton, "Jacob's War," *The Merton Seasonal*, fall 2008, 4.

86 Aelred Graham, "Thomas Merton: A Modern Man in Reverse," *Atlantic Monthly*, January 1953, 71–72.

87 *Diaries of Evelyn Waugh*, 722.

88 "Face to Face," with John Freeman, BBC, June 18, 1960.

89 Thomas Merton, *The Journals of Thomas Merton*, vol. 5, *Dancing in the Water of Life* (New York: HarperCollins, 1998), 131.

90 Evelyn Waugh, *A Bitter Trial: Evelyn Waugh and John Carmel Cardinal Heenan on the Liturgical Changes* (Curdridge, UK: St. Austin Press, 1996), 58.

91 Ibid., 71.

Amory, Mark, ed. *The Letters of Evelyn Waugh*. London: Weidenfeld & Nicolson, 1980.

"The Contemplative Life." *The Times Literary Supplement*, August 11, 1950, 505.

Cooper, David D., ed. *Thomas Merton and James Laughlin: Selected Letters*. New York: W. W. Norton, 1997.

Davie, Michael, ed. *The Diaries of Evelyn Waugh*. London: Weidenfeld & Nicolson, 1976.

Davis, Robert Murray. "Grace Beyond the Reach of Sullen Art: Waugh Edits Merton." *Journal of Modern Literature* 13, no. 1, March 1986, 163–66.

Davis, Robert Murray. "How Waugh Cut Merton." *The Month*, April 1973, 150–53.

Furlong, Monica. *Merton: A Biography*. London: Collins, 1980.

Gallagher, Donat, ed. *The Essays, Articles and Reviews of Evelyn Waugh*. London: Methuen, 1983.

Giroux, Robert. "Editing *The Seven Storey Mountain*." *America*, October 22, 1988, 273–76.

———. "Thomas Merton's Durable Mountain." *New York Times*, October 11, 1998, http://www.nytimes.com/books/98/10/11/bookend/bookend.html, accessed 9 December 2014.

Graham, Aelred. "Thomas Merton: A Modern Man in Reverse." *Atlantic Monthly*, January 1953, 70–74.

Graves, Robert, and Alan Hodge. *The Reader Over Your Shoulder: A Handbook for Writers of English Prose*. London: Jonathan Cape, 1943.

Jones, Arthur. "Literary Scamp Evelyn Waugh." *Notre Dame Magazine*, autumn 2003, http://magazine.nd.edu/news/14881-literary-scamp-evelyn-waugh/.

Ker, Ian. "Waugh the Catholic." *The Tablet*, October 18, 2003, 10–12.

Lentfoehr, Sister Thérèse. "My Meeting With Evelyn Waugh." *Evelyn Waugh Newsletter* 11, no. 1, spring 1977 http://leicester.contentdm.oclc.org/cdm/singleitem/collection/p16445coll11/id/30/rec./31, accessed 9 December 2014.

Manley, Jeffrey, and John McGinty. "'Something Entirely Unique': Evelyn Waugh's 1948–49 Tours of North America, Part I, Planning and Fact-finding." *Evelyn Waugh Newsletter* 43, no. 3, winter 2013 http://leicester.contentdm.oclc.org/cdm/landingpage/collection/p16445coll11

Manley, Jeffrey and McGinty, John. "'Something Entirely Unique': Evelyn Waugh's 1948-49 Tours of North America, Part II, The Lecture Tour," *Evelyn Waugh Newsletter* 44, no. 1, spring 2013 http://leicester.contentdm.oclc.org/cdm/singleitem/collection/p16445coll11/id/127, accessed 9 December 2014.

McDonnell, Thomas P. "Why Evelyn Waugh Worried About Merton's Prose." In *Toward An Integrated Humanity: Thomas Merton's Journey*, edited by M. Basil Pennington, 25–31. Kalamazoo, MI: Cistercian Publications, 1988.

Merton, Thomas. "Jacob's War." *The Merton Seasonal,* fall 2008, 3–8.

———. *The Journals of Thomas Merton.* Vol. 2, *Entering the Silence.* San Francisco: HarperSanFrancisco, 1996.

———. *The Journals of Thomas Merton.* Vol. 5, *Dancing in the Water of Life.* New York: HarperCollins, 1998.

———. *The Secular Journal of Thomas Merton.* New York: Image, 1959.

———. *Seeds of Contemplation.* Norfolk, CT: New Directions, 1949.

———. *The Seven Storey Mountain.* New York: Harcourt Brace Jovanovich, Harvest Edition, 1976.

———. *Waters of Silence.* London: Hollis & Carter, 1950.

———. *The Waters of Siloe.* New York: Harcourt, Brace, 1949

————. *What Are These Wounds?* Milwaukee: Bruce, 1950.

Mott, Michael. *The Seven Mountains of Thomas Merton.* New York: Houghton Mifflin, 1984.

Murray, J. Franklin, sj. "Waugh Revisited: A Reminiscence." *Evelyn Waugh Studies* 23, no. 1, spring 2012 http://evelynwaughsociety.org/wp-content/uploads/2012/09/EW_Studies_Vol_43_No_1_Spring_2012 .html, accessed 9 December 2014.

Shannon, William H. *Silent Lamp: The Thomas Merton Story.* New York: Crossroad, 1992.

Shannon, William H., and Christine Bochen, eds. *Thomas Merton: A Life in Letters.* Notre Dame, IN: Ave Maria Press, 2008.

Stannard, Martin. *Evelyn Waugh: No Abiding City 1939–1966.* London: J. M. Dent, 1992.

Waugh, Evelyn. *A Bitter Trial: Evelyn Waugh and John Carmel Cardinal Heenan on the Liturgical Changes.* Curdridge, UK: St. Austin Press, 1996.

————. *Brideshead Revisited.* London: Chapman & Hall, 1945.

————. *Sword of Honour.* Boston: Little, Brown, 1961.

Weaver, Mary Jo. "Conjectures of a Disenchanted Reader." *Horizons* 30, fall 2003, 285–96.

WHO WE ARE

Paraclete Press is a publisher of books, recordings, and DVDs on Christian spirituality. Our publishing represents a full expression of Christian belief and practice—from Catholic to Evangelical, from Protestant to Orthodox.

We are the publishing arm of the Community of Jesus, an ecumenical monastic community in the Benedictine tradition. As such, we are uniquely positioned in the marketplace without connection to a large corporation and with informal relationships to many branches and denominations of faith.

WHAT WE ARE DOING

PARACLETE PRESS BOOKS   Paraclete publishes books that show the richness and depth of what it means to be Christian. Although Benedictine spirituality is at the heart of all that we do, we publish books that reflect the Christian experience across many cultures, time periods, and houses of worship. We publish books that nourish the vibrant life of the church and its people—books about spiritual practice, formation, history, ideas, and customs.

We have several different series, including the best-selling Paraclete Essentials and Paraclete Giants series of classic texts in contemporary English; Voices from the Monastery—men and women monastics writing about living a spiritual life today; award-winning poetry; best-selling gift books for children on the occasions of baptism and first communion; and the Active Prayer Series that brings creativity and liveliness to any life of prayer.

MOUNT TABOR BOOKS   Paraclete's Mount Tabor Books series focuses on liturgical worship, art and art history, ecumenism, and the first millennium church.

PARACLETE RECORDINGS   From Gregorian chant to contemporary American choral works, our music recordings celebrate sacred choral music through the centuries. Paraclete Recordings is the record label of the internationally acclaimed choir Gloriæ Dei Cantores, praised for their "rapt and fathomless spiritual intensity" by *American Record Guide,* and the Gloriæ Dei Cantores Schola, which specializes in the study and performance of Gregorian chant. Paraclete Press is also the exclusive North American distributor of the recordings of the Monastic Choir of St. Peter's Abbey in Solesmes, France, long considered to be a leading authority on Gregorian chant.

PARACLETE VIDEO PRODUCTIONS   Our DVDs offer spiritual help, healing, and biblical guidance for life issues: grief and loss, marriage, forgiveness, anger management, facing death, and spiritual formation.

Learn more about us at our website:

www.paracletepress.com or phone us toll-free at 1.800.451.5006

Idiot Psalms
New Poems
Scott Cairns

ISBN 978-1-61261-515-8, $17.00, PAPERBACK

A new collection from one of our favorite poets. Fourteen "Idiot Psalms," surrounded by dozens of other poems.

Unquiet Vigil
New and Selected Poems
Br. Paul Quenon

ISBN 978-1-61261-560-8, $19.99, FRENCH-FLAP PAPERBACK

A collection of poems seasoned through five decades of living a monastic life, these are litanies of life, work, patience, love and prayer.

99 Psalms
SAID, translated by Mark S. Burrows

ISBN 9781612612942, $17.99, PAPERBACK

SAID's 99 Psalms are poems of praise and lament, of questioning and wondering. In the tradition of the Hebrew psalmist, they find their voice in exile, in this case one that is both existential and geographical.

Practicing Silence
New and Selected Verses
Bonnie Thurston
ISBN 978-1-61261-561-5, $19.99, PAPERBACK

This book of poems is about the spiritual life and is organized according to a monastic logic. The compact and powerful language speaks to the lifelong Christian or to the spiritual seeker.

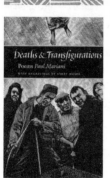

Deaths and Transfigurations
Poems
Paul Mariani
Original engravings by Barry Moser
ISBN 978-1-55725-452-8, $24.00, HARDCOVER

These spiritually searching poems develop themes of personal loss—the deaths we experience—as well as the quest for new life often known as tranfigurations.

Barry Moser, one of the world's foremost book designers and illustrators, has created a series of original engravings within the text that correspond to the major themes in Mariani's verse.

The Sea Sleeps
New and Selected Poems
Greg Miller
ISBN: 978-1-61261-427-4, $22.99, PAPERBACK

Framed by meditations on the beginnings and post-human ends of culture, the new poems reflect on the callings and limits of art in responding to desire, history, mortality, and injustice. Set in the American South, Wales, France, the Czech Republic, and Sudan, the poems address and invoke the divine.

Available from most booksellers or through Paraclete Press:
www.paracletepress.com | 1-800-451-5006
Try your local bookstore first.